Designing and Using Market Research

Robert S. Lay, *Editor*
Suffolk University

Jean J. Endo, *Editor*
University of Colorado, Boulder

NEW DIRECTIONS FOR INSTITUTIONAL RESEARCH

PATRICK T. TERENZINI, *Editor-in-Chief*
University of Georgia

MARVIN W. PETERSON, *Associate Editor*
University of Michigan

Number 54, Summer 1987

Paperback sourcebooks in
The Jossey-Bass Higher Education Series

Jossey-Bass Inc., Publishers
San Francisco • London

Robert S. Lay, Jean J. Endo (eds.).
Designing and Using Market Research.
New Directions for Institutional Research, no. 54.
Volume XIV, Number 2.
San Francisco: Jossey-Bass, 1987.

New Directions for Institutional Research
Patrick T. Terenzini, *Editor-in-Chief*
Marvin W. Peterson, *Associate Editor*

New Directions for Institutional Research is published quarterly by
Jossey-Bass Inc., Publishers (publication number USPS 098-830), and is
sponsored by the Association for Institutional Research. The volume
and issue numbers above are included for the convenience of libraries.
Second-class postage paid at San Francisco, California, and at
additional mailing offices. POSTMASTER: Send address changes to
Jossey-Bass Inc., Publishers, 433 California Street, San Francisco,
California 94104.

Editorial correspondence should be sent to the Editor-in-Chief,
Patrick T. Terenzini, Institute of Higher Education, University of
Georgia, Athens, Georgia 30602.

Library of Congress Catalog Card Number LC 85-645339

International Standard Serial Number ISSN 0271-0579

International Standard Book Number ISBN 1-55542-965-3

Cover art by WILLI BAUM

Manufactured in the United States of America

Ordering Information

The paperback sourcebooks listed below are published quarterly and can be ordered either by subscription or single copy.

Subscriptions cost $48.00 per year for institutions, agencies, and libraries. Individuals can subscribe at the special rate of $36.00 per year *if payment is by personal check.* (Note that the full rate of $48.00 applies if payment is by institutional check, even if the subscription is designated for an individual.) Standing orders are accepted.

Single copies are available at $11.95 when payment accompanies order. (California, New Jersey, New York, and Washington, D.C., residents please include appropriate sales tax.) For billed orders, cost per copy is $11.95 plus postage and handling.

Substantial discounts are offered to organizations and individuals wishing to purchase bulk quantities of Jossey-Bass sourcebooks. Please inquire.

Please note that these prices are for the academic year 1986–1987 and are subject to change without notice. Also, some titles may be out of print and therefore not available for sale.

To ensure correct and prompt delivery, all orders must give either the *name of an individual* or an *official purchase order number.* Please submit your order as follows:

> *Subscriptions:*   specify series and year subscription is to begin.
> *Single Copies:*   specify sourcebook code (such as, IR1) and first two words of title.

Mail orders for United States and Possessions, Latin America, Canada, Japan, Australia, and New Zealand to:
> Jossey-Bass Inc., Publishers
> 433 California Street
> San Francisco, California 94104

Mail orders for all other parts of the world to:
> Jossey-Bass Limited
> 28 Banner Street
> London EC1Y 8QE

New Directions for Institutional Research Series
Patrick T. Terenzini *Editor-in-Chief*
Marvin W. Peterson, *Associate Editor*

The Association for Institutional Research was created in 1966 to benefit, assist, and advance research leading to improved understanding, planning, and operation of institutions of higher education. Publication policy is set by its Publications Board.

For information about the Association for Institutional Research, write:

AIR Executive Office
314 Stone Building
Florida State University
Tallahassee, FL 32306

(904) 644-4470

Contents

Editors' Notes

Over the last ten years there has probably not been a more emotionally charged subject than that of applying the concepts and methods of marketing and market research to higher education. The issue has been before the academic community for so long that we have all gone through several stages of reactions and counterreactions.

It is safe to say that market research is here to stay; the only problem is in keeping up with its latest labels. When we do not want to bring attention to the fact that we are using a technique developed by professional managers, we disguise the activity with labels: institutional research, strategic planning, enrollment management, or one of the new labels for keeping abreast of changes in the environment—issues management. Who can argue with anything as innocuous-sounding as "issues management"? And that is part of the problem. Any institution that hopes to apply professional practices of planning to higher education should not have to resort to euphemisms when describing responses to the very real problems that higher education must face head-on: the effects of demographic changes, the uncertainties of public financing, the new demands of the world economy, and the shifts in the perceived role and value of higher education.

Higher education is influenced more by market forces than any of us would like to admit. Consider that most college students in the United States attend community colleges, which were created relatively recently to meet the escalating demand for postsecondary education outside the mold of traditional four-year colleges and universities. Yet many of the adaptations to changes since World War II have come more from increasing institutional diversity and less from changes in the way institutions are planned. In other words, most of the response to new market forces has been to graft on new programs rather than to try to adapt the old. Since we can no longer expect to deal with change through uncoordinated growth, a review of institutional mission and vitality is in order.

Academic Decision Makers and Market Researchers

Market research will not be used to maximum benefit until institutional planners know how to design and direct research that will respond to their needs. Academic decision makers are typically frustrated because most information about prospective students and about the viability of their academic programs is not very helpful. Similarly, researchers are frustrated because decision makers ask for too much and complain when that is not enough!

1

This sourcebook is an attempt to demonstate that although academic market research has not lived up to its full potential, the potential is there—if administrators create the demand for creative and useful research and are willing to invest themselves in better planning for their institutions. Market research is too important to be left to the market researchers.

In Chapter One, Larry Litten, whom we call "the conscience of the profession," provides a much-needed analysis of what should be expected from academic market research and why the field may not be realizing its potential. No one escapes the analysis unscathed—the answer is one that we do not like to hear: It is our own fault. Yet it is a little easier hearing that message from someone who has contributed so much to the field.

Research to Answer Key Policy Questions

It is not enough to criticize without giving new directions. Chapters Two through Eight provide evidence that methods exist for tackling the issues of greatest interest to college planners. At the risk of oversimplification, let us match the key policy question with the chapter that seeks to address that issue:

How Do Prospective Students View an Institution? In Chapter Two Trudy Bers describes a very useful, nonquantitative technique for understanding the perceptions of prospective students (or any other group) in their terms. This technique is exploratory and involves the observer in the thought processes of the target population.

How Does an Institution Gauge the Demand for a New or Existing Academic Program? Richard Voorhees in Chapter Three reviews several approaches that have been used successfully to assess the likelihood of success for particular academic programs to meet community and state employment needs. He also provides direction for institutions that serve wider markets with more general academic programs.

What Opportunities and Threats Are Posed by Institutions Offering Similar Academic Programs? Glenwood Rowse in Chapter Four provides a much-needed commentary on how institutions can learn more about their competitors. Not every college or university will be affected in the same way by demographic, economic, and social changes. Rowse outlines the considerations that each institution should heed in developing information on competitive shifting within overlapping markets.

How Does an Institution Position Itself to Best Advantage? Eric Straumanis offers a technique called "trade-off analysis" in Chapter Five. He illustrates how this technique may be applied to any institution or program that may be adequately described on a small number of attributes. His case is based on a popular graduate program, the MBA, within a large urban market where a number of program options exist.

What Is the Right Balance Between Tuition and the Perceived Quality of Academic Programs? In Chapter Six David Brodigan applies the technique of magnitude estimation to the measurement of perceptions and evaluations of institutional cost and quality. This is Brodigan's second major study using this technique. The approach shows great promise as an aid to planners who have found the concept of value elusive.

How Can an Institution Optimally Identify Market Segments That Correspond to a Desired Objective? There are typically hundreds of possible segments that planners might select for tailored communications. Julie Wakstein in Chapter Seven shows how a computer-assisted segmentation technique can help academic marketers explore possible combinations of characteristics to define segments in a systematic and useful way.

How Should Research Be Coordinated in an Action Plan? Market research must be directly tied to the goals and objectives established within a plan. In Chapter Eight Byron McCalmon describes the benefits of developing and implementing a marketing plan for recruiting new freshmen. McCalmon stresses the importance of involving researchers and practitioners to implement the plan successfully.

The final chapter of this sourcebook is an annotated bibliography that is a useful starting point for newcomers to academic marketing. These works provide a basic understanding of the concepts and empirical methods of market research for higher education.

Robert S. Lay
Jean J. Endo
Editors

Robert S. Lay is dean of enrollment management at Suffolk University in Boston and was director of research at Boston College for eight years.

Jean J. Endo is assistant director in the office of institutional research at the University of Colorado, Boulder. She has designed and conducted research on academic marketing, attrition, student outcomes, and alumni.

A widely acknowledged leader in this developing field reviews both the expectations and limitations of market research and concludes that only clarity of purpose will help realize the potential of the profession.

Viewing the World Without Ivy-Covered Glasses

Larry H. Litten

Market research helps us see the world more clearly and navigate our institutions effectively through complex and ever-changing markets. Although our institutions depend on these markets for survival, we often fail to give them the attention they deserve. Narcissism can be a serious affliction in academic institutions. Intellectual richness and energy abound on college campuses and can cause us to do worse than view the world through rose-colored glasses—we frequently fail to look at our markets. And when we do glance (or send our questionnaires) beyond our campus gates, we often impose *our* questions, and seek to maximize *our* interests. Good market research can overcome this kind of myopia; unfortunately, bad market research tends to reinforce it. In this chapter I want to examine some of the promise of good market research and some of the pitfalls that produce inferior market research. I will then discuss some of the exciting new developments that are occurring in this sphere and some of the further steps that we need to take to advance the craft and its contributions to more effective college administration.

Functions and Roles of Market Research

Meek and Skelly (1986, p. 33), updated St. Paul's observation of the human condition—"we see through a glass darkly"—by noting that "posi-

R. S. Lay and J. J. Endo (eds.). *Designing and Using Market Research.*
New Directions for Institutional Research, no. 54. San Francisco: Jossey-Bass, Summer 1987.

tioning an institution in the marketplace without research is like attempting to parallel park with your car windows fogged up. If you can't see where you are going—or where you have been—you are likely to bounce off a bumper or two and still not wind up where you want to be." It is a powerful image, but the image can be strengthened. Today, no institution has the luxury of parking. A more appropriate image would be trying to negotiate a crowded expressway with foggy windows. This image provides a foundation for the first of three basic observations I would like to make about market research—it is not a project or even a set of specific activities; market research is an ongoing process. It has to be ongoing because the markets it researches are dynamic entitites. But it is even more than a process; market research derives fundamentally from an attitude or a set of sensibilities. It is a defogging mechanism that allows us to see the obstacles and the opportunities that cross our institutional courses. A market research mentality impels us to ask some basic questions and to ask them periodically: What is our world like? Where do we fit into it? Where would we like to go? The answers to these questions can come from myriad sources and through an array of means.

Second, the institutions on whose behalf market research is conducted, the markets within which they operate, and the phenomena that market research seeks to study are all highly complex. Even if these elements were static, no given research project could document all the important general phenomena and relationships or unravel particular conditions and specific relationships that exist in subsets of the market. Any reasonable schematic representation of the college selection process (see for example, Hanson and Litten, 1982) makes the design of an oriental rug look like simplicity exemplified. Thus, effective market research has to be an iterative process—the answers obtained through one inquiry can only lead to questions that will need to be examined through further investigation.

Third, market research is concerned with managing or administering an institution effectively—it has to involve examination of an institution's opportunities and threats to its well-being; it has to be linked to an institution's options and decisions about them. Thus, market research has to be political to be effective. The needs felt by the people with the power to move the institution, their ways of viewing things and thinking about them, and the opportunities and constraints of the systems within which they operate have to inform both the conception and the execution of research acitivities. At the same time, the intelligence gathered by the decision makers and other members of the institution as they conduct their affairs in the market, or by people who come to us out of the market (for example, our alumni), should become part of the research data base. To be effective sources of such information, however, these agents need to be engaged directly in the development of the research. Given their frequent indispositions toward research and the demands on their time, such engagement often requires considerable ingenuity and persistence on the researcher's part.

Foci and Types of Research

The subjects of market research for a college or university—both the targets and the topics—are legion. A comprehensive, if overwhelming catalogue of market research foci is given in Kotler and Fox (1985). Smith (1986) suggests a list of three principal types of market research: (1) *exploratory research,* in which an institution seeks to understand the nature of the market and submarkets within it, and how the institution is positioned in the market; (2) *developmental research,* in which the researcher tests marketing initiatives prior to their full-scale implementation; and (3) *evaluative research,* which assesses the effectiveness of an institution's marketing activities. A comprehensive listing of *specific questions* that an institution can address via market research, especially in the exploratory mode, has been developed by Davis–Van Atta and Carrier (1986).

Insufficiencies and Constraints in Current Practice

Market research in higher education has progressed mightily in the past decade. This development has often occurred in the face of adverse forces. These forces can impede individual researchers and research projects. Further progress for academic market research as a field of endeavor could be slowed or arrested if these forces are not contained and overcome. I note these research demons here because researchers will need to guard against them if they are to produce effective market research. As a profession we also have a collective responsibility to work through our associations to banish these adverse forces from the realm, or at least to contain the damage they inflict on our capacities to do our jobs well.

Low Levels of Resources. Compared to expenditure levels outside of higher education, academic market research appears to be generally underfunded. I can only say "appears to be" because we lack data on the scale of market research activities in higher education, and drawing direct comparisons with other sectors is difficult due to the differing modes of operation. Business and industry spend vast sums on market research and purchase both powerful intellectual resources and extensive field work to achieve their ends. The most recent of the periodic studies conducted by the American Marketing Association on market research expenditures indicates that consumer goods companies spend a median of 0.65 to 0.30 percent of their sales volume (dollars) on market research, depending on the size of the company (expenditures as a percent of sales are inversely related to sales volume); financial services companies spend 0.70 to 0.10 percent of sales volume (Twedt, 1983). To the extent that educational and general expenditures are a proxy for sales volume (and the comparison is problematic), these median rates would translate into an annual market research program of $90,000–$100,000 for a college or university with a $25 million budget. And beyond the private expenditures of companies for research lie the large sums spent on research by trade associations and the extensive corporate support for basic market research in schools of business—phenomena that have no equivalent in higher education. Nevertheless, in spite of the lack of data for our industry and the difficulty of making comparative judgments even if data did exist, we can note that a very small cadre in the Association for Institutional Research attends the annual meetings of its special-interest group on market research (approximately thirty to forty people). We can observe the hint of horror that creeps into conversations with academic administrators when the costs of some of the more primitive market research projects that are routine in business are quoted in conjunction with institutional proposals for market research. Low-budget research can often be creative and imaginative. More often, however, it fails to get the job done right, which leads to disappointments with the results, challenges to the findings, or enervation of the researchers. Dissatisfaction with research results can establish a deadly cycle in which funding for further research is withheld or given too sparingly.

Institutional researchers can combat this demon in several ways: We can decline to carry out projects that are insufficiently funded. We can seek ways of combining our efforts and our resources with those of other parties in consortial execution of some of the higher-risk projects of interest and in pursuit of data on common problems. We can attempt to exploit the research models developed outside of higher education in order to save the time and effort involved in reinventing them.

Misdirected or Inflated Expectations. Administrators often turn to research as a last-ditch effort in the face of severe institutional problems or unresolvable administrative dilemmas. They expect the relatively inexperienced and conservative people in their market to provide inspiration and direction regarding services to be offered, pricing, and so forth that can come only from professional imagination and judgment based on appropriate information. They often expect clear and definitive answers to very complex questions about highly elusive phenomena. And they expect these results to come via rather primitive resrach tools. At the same time, academic administrators are often the victims of researchers who promise the delivery of just such a set of impossible outcomes. Expecting more than a research project can reasonably deliver is a guarantee of disappointment and the negative consequences that follow such disappointments.

Administrators and indeed, researchers, often expect precise answers to vague questions (for example, elaborate research projects undertaken on the basis of nothing more than a vague desire to "find out how we are viewed in the market"—projects that are often the result of trustee interest or support or are undertaken in response to the availability of foundation funding). But vague questions rarely produce sharp answers. At the other extreme, administrators are often interested only in questions that lead directly to action (and will go so far as to employ that abominable term— *actionable data*). But some of our circumstances, for example, the way in which people evaluate the locations of some institutions, cannot be altered. Nevertheless, we need to understand such intractable problems in order to know how hard we will have to work on other fronts to compensate for conditions we cannot change.

Administrators also complain that research reports only the obvious or confirms what we already know. At times this is true, but all knowledge should be subjected to periodic confirmation, especially under changing conditions, and private knowledge should be forced to become public knowledge if it is to constitute the basis for institutional policy. Research can do this, not only via its results, but through participation in its design.

Market research is often better at clarifying the questions or the issues, sometimes even bringing the options into greater relief, than it is at providing definitive answers. It is certainly better at *testing* new ideas than it is at *generating* them. The usefulness of the research is often a function of the specificity of the questions asked (which does not suggest that the *focus* of the inquiry should be narrow and overlook important aspects of complex phenomena). Inevitably, professional imagination (often in the form of theory or hypotheses) is required to give research focus and to wrest directives for action from its findings. Market researchers should be encouraged to present their proposals for research as elements in a process of ongoing inquiry, acknowledging that more work is likely to follow any given project. We need to respond to requests for information and guidance by offering to help clarify issues, not to deliver answers. Research thus conceived can be an invaluable stimulus to innovation and initiatives; research that is expected or purported to do more is more likely to be a depressant.

Insularity. Academic institutions and the academic professions are rich in intellectual resources—both ideas and interesting people. We often get caught up in, even overwhelmed by, these resources and fail to consider that the world of insights and imagination does not stop at our campus gates or at the boundaries of our disciplines. We suffer insularity on three counts: (1) as members of a particular administrative team and a particular professional community; (2) as practitioners of market research within institutions of higher education; and (3) as practitioners of research grounded in the social sciences.

Institutions of higher education can operate as almost total institutions—we gain not only our economic and professional rewards from these institutions but we often get many cultural and social benefits from them as well. Our identities become bound up with these institutions, and our research foci show the effects. We often go into the market simply to find out how we are viewed and what people would like from us. All too often we fail to ask hard, searching, and wide-ranging questions about how our institution stacks up against the options that students have for achieving their objectives—that is, the competition, or more precisely, our specific competitors. Two common indicators of such myopia are specifications of institutional "position" that focus simply on viewbook-like statements of generic characteristics (for example, "we are small, dedicated to teaching, with a concern for all aspects of personal development. . . .") and research that gets detailed ratings of the sponsoring institution but not of competitors (or at best, competitor ratings that are from a biased subset of people in the market such as our cross-applicants).

A wealth of theory, empirical data, and case studies exists in the realm of marketing as developed and practiced outside of higher education. Faculty and administrators who rose through faculty ranks often suffer from an arrogance concerning the value of nonacademic activities and a sense of superiority over people who deal with the making of money. These attitudes have not failed to infect many others who labor in academic institutions. We ignore developments in the secular world of marketing, however, to our own detriment. As noted earlier, the sums of money available for market research in the commercial world have purchased some substantial intellectual power and provided the wherewithall to engage in extensive research of remarkable variety. Some of the theory, findings, and practices developed in nonacademic marketing are not applicable to higher education (for example, product life-cycles fail to describe adequately either the enduring nature of many liberal arts "products" or the very brief "life-cycle" of a given course or major that needs constant reengineering to stay current with the state of its field and to relate to the varied educational needs of its students). Much of this secular wisdom requires substantial adaption if it is to be useful in higher education (for example, simplistic positioning theory based on a single product or product line does not work well for complex institutions with many programs that fit together in intricate ways to produce multiple outcomes or benefits). Nevertheless, these intellectual resources can provide immense stimulation for imagination and initiatives in our sphere. Many research techniques, however, are readily imported without much modification or require only minor adapations.

Insularity also results from grounding our inquiries in the methods and data of the social sciences. I would not seek to diminish the importance of this tradition or suggest that it will not continue to be basic to our enterprise. However, as we seek to understand people, their educational needs, and their behavior related to these needs, much of value can be found beyond our questionnaires and interviews. For example, the insights afforded by the authors of fiction can in some ways be richer and more powerful than the data we gather by quantitative methods. These students of the human condition and behavior can point our quantitative inquiries in new directions, and they can provide compelling examples with which we can illustrate our findings. But how many of us read novels about late adolescence and the concerns of adolescents in conjunction with our research on traditional students and the ways they view educational issues or colleges?

Insularity will be overcome only by movement across boundaries— by regularly comparing our institutions with our competitors' in our research and in our thinking about ourselves; by reading the literature of the secular marketing world, attending its professional meetings, and inviting market researchers to make presentations at our meetings; and by reading outside of the social sciences. Given the work loads and deadlines under which we often labor, such reaching out can be difficult indeed. But in the long run it can be both refreshing and the source of greater productivity.

Proprietary Attitudes. One of the greatest impediments to the free flow of ideas is the sense of proprietary ownership that comes when personal advantage is expected to flow from an idea. Business is notorious for keeping its research classified (the fact that there is a substantial secular market research literature is testimony to the abundance of such activity, for we see only the tip of the iceberg). Along with the marketing theory and research techniques that we have imported from business, we have also become vulnerable to the poison of proprietary attitudes toward our own research. As often as not, the problem lies not with the researcher but with administrators who seek exclusvie exploitation of information for personal or institutional ends by restricting its dissemination. But this behavior runs directly counter to traditional academic attitudes governing the free flow of information. Not only is such behavior damaging in its own right but it establishes a precedent by which we may treat other ideas in a proprietary manner because they might be to an institution's advantage. Should this happen, we will no longer be academic institutions, and the intellectual function in our society will be severely compromised. More is at stake than the quality of our market research.

Our research will also limp along, however, if we cannot learn from each other's mistakes and successes. We need to recognize that market research is an intellectual activity, just like other research. Although it has its practical elements, even its practical foundations, often it does not result in immediate practical results—it simply helps provide the framework in which such results are eventually realized. Researchers require the criticism and confirmation of their peers in order to achieve a sense of professional respectability and fulfillment and to develop their craft (see Storer, 1966, for a discussion of the essential role that criticism plays in any intellectual activity). Administrators who suppress this element of the researcher's life do violence to the professional well-being of the individual researcher and to the intellectual class to which he or she belongs.

A free sharing of techniques and findings is the only defense against this demon. This is not to say that proprietary interests are not involved in market research or that institutions should be precluded from deriving practical advantage from the conduct of research. One of the reasons so much money is given to the research enterprise in the business world is because it does bring returns of such proprietary advantage. However, reasonable temporal limits should be placed on the restraint of research dissemination, and administrators should actively encourage publication after sufficient time has passed to solidify any immediate institutional advantages the research produces.

Professional Elitism. The final demon to be addressed is one over which the individual researcher has considerable power. It can be an arrogance toward the subjects or toward the users of our research or both. It is manifested in a refusal to speak the language of either group or to live within the frames of reference used by members of the group.

In the design of our research on students, we often ask the questions that we want answered in the ways that make sense to us. Students, especially the amiable ones who have not been refined in the intellectual smelters of academia, will answer our questions regardless of whether they address issues that are meaningful to them or are phrased in a manner that is most appropriate to the ways in which they think and view things. Although our survey questions are often thoughtful and well considered and frequently well worked-over in committees, there is no reason to believe that the world view of academics addresses the world of students in their terms. And it is in *their world* and *in their own terms* that they will be forming their views, making their decisions, and consequently affecting our lives and our institutions. We frequently fail to listen attentively to students or to watch them carefully before we start asking the particular questions in our surveys that generate the data that we push through our quantitative analyses and models. Our failure is due in part to time and resource constraints, but it is in part a failure to treat our subjects with the full respect they deserve, not only as human beings but as the people with the real power in the marketplace.

At the other end of the research process, we frequently fail to work within the frames of reference of the decision makers who seek insights via our research. At our best, we may pose interesting problems and ask interesting questions, but they are not necessarily the problems or the questions that bear directly on the decisions faced by policy makers and administrators. And we frequently fail to place ourselves, or to try to imagine ourselves, in the roles or with the responsibilities of the users of research. Achieving these perspectives often takes more than simply asking these users what they want to know; it frequently requires that *we* provide the major part of the energy required to bridge the gap between practice and inquiry, that *we* identify with and project ourselves into the sphere of the administrator, that *we* formulate the research within the context of the marketer's practical concerns, and that *we* propose decisions acknowledging their limitations but helping to take the unavoidable risks. We also need to talk about our research in language that has meaning to administrators. The research should be as quantitatively sophisticated as required to get solid evidence on the issues we address; our presentations, however, should recognize that many administrators in higher education, especially the marketers (admissions and development officers), have been trained as humanists without quantitative backgrounds, and others, though trained in the social sciences, do not have sophisticated knowledge of quantitative methods. If we want to communicate effectively with these users, we must speak in a language familiar to them. We may have to translate our numbers into stories, tell anecdotes, or present effective graphics. We do not need to talk down to our nonresearch colleagues; we simply need to stop talking past them as often as we do. We need to read (and reread) authorities on good writing (such as Zinsser, 1980, and Newman, 1974) and take pains to practice what they preach.

Promising Developments in Higher Education Market Research

In spite of the forces that could work against a full flowering of market research in higher education, the field exhibits a respectable state of development. Credit is due to the initiative and dedication of a small cadre of workers. Furthermore, some recent developments suggest the possibility of a more exciting future. Within higher education, greatly expanded levels and types of attention to market research should produce some major advances (provided proprietary attitudes do not unduly constrain the sharing of experiences—and this volume is an indication that antidotes to this poison do exist). Outside of higher education, the rapid escalation of attention that marketers are giving explicitly to the particular problems of marketing *services* will contribute substantially to our reservoir of theory and empirical data (provided we overcome the affliction of insularity).

The publication of market research in higher education has increased enormously in recent years. The College Entrance Examination Board publishes *The Admissions Strategist* twice a year. It contains articles on market research sprinkled among the descriptions of marketing activities that constitute its principal fare. A more frequent, albeit more pricey, newsletter with similar foci, *College Marketing Alert,* is published by Capitol Publications. The Council for the Advancement and Support of Education (CASE) carries brief articles on marketing (with some attention to market research) in its *CASE Currents* magazine, and these articles have been collected in *The New Guide to Student Recruitment Marketing* (Smith and Hunt, 1986). Other professional journals such as *Journal of Higher Education, College and University,* and *Research in Higher Education* have expanded somewhat the amount of space they give to research on college marketing topics. Presentations at professional meetings (the various associations for institutional researchers, admissions officers, and development officers) continue to include a smattering of market research papers, some of which eventually end up in the publications just mentioned.

The College Entrance Examination Board has undertaken an important initiative in the provision of services to colleges that will advance their understanding of the market and marketing processes. Its Enrollment Planning Service (EPS) broke new ground by providing institutions with ways of estimating their shares of specific geographical markets, projecting future draws from those markets in the context of their demographic conditions, and searching for promising new markets. Although the data base has its limitations (it is tied to the submission of SAT scores to institutions and not to actual applications; it does not permit critical ways of segmenting the data by, for example, ability or income; and single-year snapshots can be misleading, especially for small colleges), the EPS fosters a relatively sophisticated perspective on the market and provides data not available through other means (the American College Testing Service offers a more rudimentary service of this type, which can help fill in some of the gaps created by the particular geographical distribtution of SAT data).

A new resource of immense value to small private colleges is the ongoing grant program of the Consortium for the Advancement of Private Higher Education (CAPHE). This program, funded by several foundations, offers matching grants of up to $50,000 in four program areas, one of which is strategic planning, with another focused on market research projects. As the first round of grants under this program is completed, CAPHE has also initiated dissemination of the methods and results of projects in these areas.

A number of consortiums have recently undertaken market research on behalf of their members. These activities address issues common to the institutions, and they spread both the costs and the risks of such research across a broader financial base. Since formal market research is usually expensive and is inherently risky (whether anything of immediate practical value will be learned is not ensured), this cooperative device holds great promise for getting research done and enhancing its value through broadbased discussion of its findings. Notable among these consortial efforts are the projects undertaken by the Women's College Coalition, the Christian College Coalition (small denominational colleges), and the Consortium on the Financing of Higher Education (selective, private, national institutions).

Outside of higher education, the emergence of a subfield that focuses on the marketing of services (as contrasted with the marketing of goods) within the marketing profession should provide substantial benefits for higher education (see Litten, 1986, for a discussion of some of the concepts and principles of services marketing). Several specific developments in this area promise to be of value to higher education: The American Marketing Association sponsors a newsletter and meetings that focus specifically on services; the Wharton School of the University of Pennsylvania and Arizona State University have each established services-marketing research centers (with the latter supporting an electronic bibliography of services marketing and offering short seminars on services marketing topics); and the Marketing Science Institute in Cambridge, Massachusetts, has a new program on services marketing.

Needed Developments in Higher Education Market Research

Market research in higher education is well established, and it continues to be carried forward despite the several obstacles enumerated in this chapter. Much remains to be done, however, before the field fully matures. In addition to removal of the impediments I have listed, several other developments would move us forward in large increments. Some of these are undertakings too large for any individual or institution; they are endeavors with a set of benefits too broad to be either captured or underwritten by private (individual or institutional) interests. I mention them here because they are important in our collective lives, even though attending to such concerns necessarily distracts from the immediate interests and reward structures in which an individual institutional researcher is embedded. The associations to which we belong (and the leaders who guide them), the sabbaticals that we take (all too infrequently), and the periodic sense of vision and professional responsibility that lifts us beyond our immediate concerns could each focus on one or more of these developments and provide the energy to carry them forward.

First, we need closer ties to the secular world of marketing beyond higher education. We need to keep abreast of the marketing literature; attend the professional meetings of marketing associations, the marketing seminars, and the lectures sponsored by the departments of our business schools (for those of us in institutions that have them); engage marketing faculty in cooperative research projects (or luncheon conversations or whatever gets us together). We need not be defensive or supplicatory in our posture toward the members of the marketing profession (they misunderstand the nature and concerns of higher education as frequently as they get it right, and we have things to teach, especially concerning the marketing of ongoing relationships), but we need to be aggressive in seeking out what they have and adapting it to our needs and goals.

Second, we need to develop the functional equivalent of the marketing research activities that occur in business schools and research centers like the Marketing Science Institute, the Strategic Planning Institute, or even the trade associations. These agents carry on enormous amounts of basic, nonproprietary research on consumer behavior, market structures, and organizations' marketing performances. This work benefits all the members of a class of marketing entities (for example, the firms in an industry), and it is research that permits each marketer to develop much more effective market research for his or her own firm. Business supports this research quite handsomely. Colleges and universities need to encourage and support our trade associations (national and state associations that represent and serve a given type of institution, for example, private or public colleges and universities, liberal arts colleges, community colleges, and denominational colleges) to do the same. We need to engage the business school faculty to pursue such endeavors or create joint research centers supported by schools of business and schools of education.

We should also exploit the extensive resources that could be placed at our disposal by trustees and alumni who are well placed in firms that have extensive marketing research expertise. Personnel from corporate market research departments can provide valuable consulting services, especially from corporations or agencies in the service sector of the economy; for the traditional college, corporations for which the youth market is important would be especially appropriate resources. Even better, administrative sabbaticals spent in such a setting could provide invaluable professional development opportunities for institutional researchers. At the least, committees that advise on institutional marketing policy or on major market research projects could benefit from the inclusion of trustees and alumni with strong marketing expertise.

Finally, we need more and better opportunities for presenting the fruits of our marketing research labors. There is currently a very wide gap between the frequently superficial presentations of market research that abound in the literature directed primarily at academic marketers (admissions or development officers) and the frequently pedestrian and turgid research presentations in professional publications. The type of information contained in this New Directions volume is precisely what is needed to fill in this gap. But we need more of this kind of undertaking. It will happen, however, only if we find more people who have this kind of information to share and who are willing to take the time to prepare it for presentation (and to obtain the blessings of their employers to expend effort in this way).

References

Davis-Van Atta, D. L., and Carrier, S. C. "Using the Institutional Research Office." In D. Hossler (ed.), *Managing College Enrollments.* New Directions for Higher Education, no. 53. San Francisco: Jossey-Bass, 1986.

Hanson, K., and Litten, L. H. "Mapping the Road to Academe: A Review of Research on Women, Men, and the College Selection Process." In P. Perun (ed.), *The Undergraduate Woman: Issues in Educational Equity.* Lexington, Mass.: Lexington Books, 1982.

Kotler, P., and Fox, K.F.A. *Strategic Marketing for Educational Institutions.* Englewood Cliffs, N.J.: Prentice-Hall, 1985.

Litten, L. H. "Perspectives on Pricing." In D. Hossler (ed.), *Managing College Enrollments.* New Directions for Higher Education, no. 53. San Francisco: Jossey-Bass, 1986.

Meek, E., and Skelly, G. "Defog with Research." In V. C. Smith and S. Hunt (eds.), *The New Guide to Student Recruitment Marketing.* Washington, D.C.: Council for the Advancement and Support of Education, 1986.

Newman, E. *Strictly Speaking.* Indianapolis, Ind.: Bobbs-Merrill, 1974.

Smith, R. "Knowledge Is Power." In V. C. Smith and S. Hunt (eds.), *The New Guide to Student Recruitment Marketing.* Washington, D.C.: Council for the Advancement and Support of Education, 1986.

Smith, V. C., and Hunt, S. (eds.). *The New Guide to Student Recruitment Marketing.* Washington, D.C.: Council for the Advancement and Support of Education, 1986.

Storer, N. W. *The Social System of Science.* New York: Holt, Rinehart & Winston, 1966.

Twedt, D. *1983 Survey of Marketing Research.* Chicago: American Marketing Association, 1983.

Zinsser, W. *On Writing Well.* New York: Harper & Row, 1980.

Larry H. Litten is associate director and director of research at the Consortium on Financing Higher Education, Cambridge, Massachusetts.

The exploration of institutional images is an emotionally charged task often given to researchers. The focus group methodology exposes the richness and complexity of feelings and perceptions.

❀

Exploring Institutional Images Through Focus Group Interviews

Trudy H. Bers

Market research in higher education can benefit greatly by using qualitative methods to generate new insights and provide a deeper understanding of perceptions and behaviors. This chapter shows how focus group interviews are appropriately used in market research. It describes their implementation, and it discusses their benefits and drawbacks. Briefly, focus group interviewing is a qualitative research technique in which a small number of respondents—generally eight to ten—and a moderator participate in an unstructured group discussion about selected subjects. A typical discussion session lasts for one to two hours. Focus group interviews elicit in-depth, albeit subjective, information to help researchers understand the deeply held perceptions of students or other groups of policy importance to a college or university. The method is best used to identify attitudinal dimensions and not to quantify the extent to which these are held in any population or subgroup.

A growing body of literature describes the processes and uses of focus group interviews in a variety of settings. Few articles, however, are grounded in research theory. An exception is Calder (1977), who provides a typology from a philosophy-of-science perspective. Calder suggests that

R. S. Lay and J. J. Endo (eds.). *Designing and Using Market Research.*
New Directions for Institutional Research, no. 54. San Francisco: Jossey-Bass, Summer 1987.

focus group interviews can be characterized by three general types of approaches. The first approach is exploratory, to generate hypotheses and constructs for subsequent testing using quantitative research techniques or to help confirm the results of earlier quantitative research. The second approach is clinical; here focus group interviews are undertaken to understand the "real" underlying causes of behavior detected through the "clinical judgment" of specially trained moderators. The third approach is phenomenological, to help researchers or other observers intuitively know and understand how individuals in the group experience their world, to see the world through the respondents' eyes without evaluating the accuracy or correctness of that view. Calder argues that each approach necessitates different decisions with regard to such aspects of focus group interviewing as selecting the moderator, selecting the respondents, conducting the discussion sessions, and using the results.

Hess (1968) presents the relative advantages of focus group interviews as compared to individual, in-depth interviews. Among the advantages to the respondent are synergism, that is when a group's combined effort will produce more than the sum of individual responses; snowballing, the process by which one person's comment triggers a chain of responses from others; stimulation; security; and spontaneity. Advantages also accrue to the sponsor of the research. These include serendipity, when an idea pops out spontaneously; specialization, in the case of using a well-trained moderator who would be too expensive to use for individual interviews; scientific scrutiny, available through direct observation of a group or a tape of its session; structure, obtained through the control exerted by a moderator; and speed.

Langer (1986) provides guidelines for conducting qualitative research and reminds researchers not to be surprised when respondents are inconsistent, different from model or idealized subjects in the population being studied, uncaring about a college or university, angry about some aspect of an institution, or uninformed. Goldman and McDonald (1987) will soon publish a book on the principles and practices of focus group interviews, and Higgenbotham and Cox (1979) provide a variety of research examples. Many other articles and books about focus group interviews are available, the majority of which are recent—testimony to the relatively new status of focus group interviewing as a viable and appropriate market research technique.

Initial Planning of Focus Group Studies

As with any good research method, focus group interviews entail more planning and thought than is immediately apparent to those who think of it as simply a couple of hours of informal group discussion. In this section and the next, I examine the elements of a successful focus group study. Examples are drawn from focus group marketing research using adult students conducted at Oakton College in spring 1986 (Bers and Smith-Bandy, 1986).

General Approach and Specific Purpose. Before conducting a focus group study, it is important to clarify the general research approach. Calder's typology may be useful here. The specific purpose of a focus group study must also be clearly identified. Among the possible purposes related to market research in higher education are the following: to investigate the perceptions of an institution by constituent groups such as potential students, parents of potential students, and high school counselors and teachers; to examine the evaluations by potential recipients of college brochures, other promotional materials, and alternative marketing campaigns; and to generate new ideas for improving or adding services (such as advisement, registration, and child-care).

To clarify the approach and purpose of a focus group study, researchers need to discuss these issues with relevant college personnel. It is important that a consensus be achieved before proceeding further if the research is to be successful. The approach and purpose of a study will determine most of the other aspects of the design and conduct of the research.

The Oakton College study was undertaken to generate hypotheses for a future quantitative study of college choice and evaluations and to get in touch with or learn more about the phenomenology of nontraditional students. Its purpose was to examine the college choice decision-making processes of adult students and their impressions and attitudes about Oakton College's programs and services. While many factors affected the decision to use focus group interviews in this study, the most important was that no one at Oakton College had consciously talked to nontraditional students to ask about their experiences in selecting the college or evaluating its programs and services.

Respondents. Once the general approach and specific purpose of a focus group study have been determined, appropriate respondents must be recruited. Researchers should be aware that if care in recruiting respondents is not taken, the accuracy and usefulness of information will be compromised. Depending on the specific study and the nature of the institution, various criteria will probably need to be followed to ensure that respondents are members of the populations of interest. For example, a selective college wishing to conduct research on potential students will want to ensure that respondents meet minimum academic standards for admission. Also, having participated in other focus group interviews ought not by itself to disqualify a potential respondent.

A question related to recruiting respondents is whether livelier or more perceptive discussions arise in groups that are heterogeneous or homogeneous in the characteristics qualifying respondents for inclusion. In general, the more researchers wish to understand a group's shared perspective (the phenomenological approach), the more important it is that the group be homogeneous. When the approach is exploratory, heterogeneity is more acceptable.

The Oakton College study used recently enrolled women and men who were age twenty-five or over during their first terms at Oakton College and who had earned at least fifteen credits. This was done so that the discussion sessions would consist of students who were familiar with and had shown some commitment to the college. Separate sessions for women and men were conducted, but there was no attempt to differentiate by such factors as major, age, or credits earned.

For some types of focus group studies, researchers might well look to college employees as potential respondents as well as to those outside the institution. For example, an institution that wishes to generate ideas about improving the way in which it presents itself to campus visitors might conduct focus group interviews with employees such as security guards, maintenance personnel, and receptionists and secretaries. They will be familiar with problems and can offer insights into possible solutions from very different perspectives than their supervisors. Improved commitment to the institution and higher morale are additional positive effects generated by employee participation.

Moderator. Once the approach, the purpose, and the respondents have been decided on, a moderator's guide needs to be prepared. Such a guide lists important topics to be covered in a discussion session and may even contain suggested questions to ensure that important terminology is included and relevant points are probed. It is important to remember, however, that the guide is just that, and not a structured questionnaire or interview schedule. One of the primary benefits of focus group interviewing is that it allows researchers to explore and obtain elaborations on subjects pertinent to a study but not anticipated in advance.

A skilled moderator familiar with the study should be able to cover virtually all of the issues in the guide yet take advantage of new subjects that arise spontaneously. When a study includes more than one group, all topics will not be discussed in every group, since the natural flow of conversation might make introducing some topics too artificial or even divert a group from a more fruitful line of discussion. If it is imperative to cover certain topics or questions with a group, the moderator should be made aware of this in advance. A moderator normally does some combination of the following in a discussion session (Mariampolski, 1984):

- Rapport building, in which the moderator establishes rapport with the respondents and orients them to the general task at hand.
- Exploration, in which very general questions are posed such as, "What comes to mind when I mention XYZ College?" or "What do you think of when you imagine your ideal college?"

- Probing, in which the moderator narrows the discussion for elaboration on specific topics and introduces new issues to expand the discussion.
- Closing, in which respondents are given a final opportunity to add to the discussion by answering such general questions as, "Is there anything else you want to say about XYZ College?"

Other things that might be added include task accomplishment, in which respondents are to be asked to perform a task such as ranking suggested promotional themes, and evaluation, in which respondents are asked to evaluate such test items as brochures and advertising designs.

While most respondents are cooperative and expressive, moderators must be prepared to cope with those who are unusually verbose, hostile, passive, or obnoxious. Bers and Smith-Bandy (1986) have categorized such respondents and offered suggestions for dealing with them:

- Ax-grinder, who dwells on a very negative experience. The moderator should say that a particular concern has been heard and need not be repeated, and avoid eye contact to discourage repeated discussion.
- Self-styled expert, who claims absolute knowledge. The moderator must weigh the benefit of correcting misinformation with the risk of discouraging participation from others who fear they will be corrected if their comments are "wrong."
- Single-issue respondent, who fixates on a topic. The moderator should treat this person as an ax-grinder, but may need to make direct statements that the single issue in question is not on the group's agenda.
- Adviser, who tells the college how to improve, but whose ideas are in fact trite and have probably been implemented already or are impossible. The moderator must tolerate this, lest others be discouraged from offering their ideas.
- Special case, who deviates from the norm, often through aberrant behavior or perceptions. If possible, known cases should be screened out unless there is a real interest in talking to them. Outside moderators may not recognize the special case.
- Nonparticipant, who attends but doesn't talk. The moderator should use smiles, nods of approval, and even gentle but direct invitations to participate.

Number of Groups. A frequent concern is how many different groups of respondents to include in a single study. One rule of thumb is to hold at least two groups to reduce the chances of an atypical group providing all the input. A second rule of thumb is to continue to hold sessions until virtually the same discussion is repeated. If a study is being done to brainstorm ideas, however, one group might suffice, regardless of how atypical the respondents appear.

Conducting Focus Group Studies

After initial planning, several decisions related to the actual implementation of a focus group study must be made. There are few right or wrong decisions; rather, such factors as those just described as well as the resources and time available will influence the way in which a study is conducted.

Location. Typically discussion sessions are held in small rooms equipped with a conference table and comfortable chairs or couches. Hot and cold drinks and, depending on the time of day, snacks or a light meal are provided. Sessions are generally taped, and, when watching the reactions of respondents to physical or visual materials is important, videotaping is recommended. Commercial focus group facilities, of which there are more than seven hundred, also provide a viewing room for observers (which is of course necessary only if observers are part of a study). The viewing room is behind one-way glass and enables a person to watch a session in progress. Respondents should be told they are being taped or observed; there is generally no resistance or effect on their behavior, since taping equipment is unobtrusive and observers cannot be seen.

Observers. It has become common practice for representatives of a college or university to observe discussion sessions. This is not necessarily important, however, particularly when a study's general approach is to explore new ideas rather than to provide decision makers with a "feel" for the kinds of people in whom they are interested. When observers are present and they are unfamiliar with focus group interviews, there is a tendency for them to jump to conclusions or target a particular phase or idea as a generalizable finding. One way to discourage this is for the study director to hold an immediate debriefing with observers at the conclusion of each session to permit them to share their first reactons and be gently reminded of the ways in which the results might be properly and improperly used. When focus group interviews are held at locations some distance from an institution, observers' travel costs and time away from their offices can add significantly to the study's costs.

Moderator. Moderators are either selected from college personnel or hired from outside. If a study is following an exploratory or clinical approach, the moderator should have some scientific training (Calder, 1977). Regardless of the approach, it is imperative that the moderator understand the research so that he or she can appropriately select statements to probe and further explore topics, guide the discussion away from irrelevant issues, and take advantage of spontaneous or unexpected comments that are germane to the project. At a minimum, the moderator needs to be a good communicator who puts respondents at ease and encourages them to share their ideas candidly. The moderator should also be empathetic and capable of participating without biasing the results or leading respondents, and he or she must be able to provide the college or university with insightful observations (Welch, 1985).

Skillful moderators rely on numerous tactics to draw out reticent respondents and to prevent those with strong personalities from dominating a discussion session. For example, useful statements to elicit comments include, "I'm interested in your thoughts on that, Joe," "That's an interesting observation, Joe; will you elaborate a bit?" and "Can you tell us more about that?" Encouraging cues also include nods of the head, "um hums," and repeating statements as preludes to the next question. Tactics to discourage overbearing respondents include statements such as, "Will you hold that thought for a minute, Joe? I want to hear the rest of what Jane is saying," or "Let's listen to Jane, now." Avoiding eye contact, the implicit signal that permission to speak is being granted, and refusing to call on someone also aid in maintaining control.

Use of Service Provider. Commercial firms provide an array of services for planning, implementing, and analyzing focus group studies. Among such services (each, of course, for a fee) are providing a facility, recruiting respondents, making reminder phone calls or mailings, hiring a moderator, arranging refreshments for the respondents and observers, providing audio and visual tapes, preparing a written summary and analysis of the results, and writing thank you letters. The extent to which commercial firms are used will be influenced by the nature of a study and the availability of resources, including the ability of a college's researchers to conduct the discussion sessions.

Respondents. Identifying and recruiting respondents is one of the most important elements in a successful focus group study. Often the suitability of respondents is not clear until a discussion session is underway. To improve the suitability of respondents for a study, various screening or qualifying criteria are generally employed. For example, a college interested in exploring its image among prospective students may draw respondents from its inquiry pool, assuming that these persons have at least heard of the institution. If there is concern about the size and quality of the inquiry pool, then respondents might be drawn from lists of high school juniors or seniors whose test scores indicate they would qualify for admission. In short, random selection of respondents is often unwise, since persons selected in this way usually have little to contribute. While some qualifying of respondents is recommended, applying stringent criteria will increase a study's costs if many contacts are needed before a sufficient number of qualified respondents can be recruited.

Because respondents are being asked to devote several hours of their time and must perhaps travel to a special site, incentives are usually provided. Generally $25 is considered an adequate sum, though some studies pay as much as $100 to $150 to professionals or others who are difficult to recruit. The issue of monetary incentives is especially sensitive for public institutions whose administrations and boards are reluctant to allocate public funds for this purpose. Nevertheless, incentives may be essential for recruiting respondents and should be considered as analogous to printing and postage costs in a mail survey; they are simply part of the cost of doing research.

Analysis and Presentation of Results

As with any research, the results of a focus group study must be analyzed. One common format is to identify broad themes that emerged in the discussion sessions and then to elaborate somewhat on each. For example, in the Oakton College study, several themes were identified from the four sessions conducted with returning women students, and these were described in detail. Returning women, for instance, did not engage in careful consideration of alternative colleges. Rather, they decided to return to school *and* to Oakton College as one decision, and they based this overwhelmingly on the Oakton College's convenience. Only after they were enrolled did these students begin to asssess the quality of the faculty or their choice of programs.

The results of a focus group study are usually presented in two types of reports. One type of provides a general overview of findings, including brief sections on the nature of the research, recruitment and characteristics of respondents, and major themes that emerged. The second type is more extensive and includes numerous verbatim comments. Because results are qualitative in nature, neither type of report includes statistics; instead, terms like *some* and *most* are used.

Benefits and Drawbacks of Focus Group Interviews

Focus group interviews are an effective research method, but they are not without problems. The following are among their primary benefits. First, focus group interviews enable college officials to observe people who may be very different from themselves as well as different from idealized or stereotyped models (Dickenson, 1986). For example, admissions directors may think of potential students as being goal-directed and knowledgeable about the college search process. Mail or telephone surveys that elicit responses to multiple-choice questions often perpetuate this image. Focus group interviews, however, may well reveal that potential students are disorganized, use irrational or very subjective reasons for selecting particular institutions, and know very little about college majors.

A second benefit of focus group interviews is their potential use as morale boosters when college personnel are involved as respondents (Fram, 1985). Since college staff members often possess critical information that is not systematically collected and may even feel ignored, inviting them to participate in focus group interviews serves both to obtain their ideas and to improve morale. A third benefit of focus group interviews is that they enable college personnel who are involved as observers to hear the language and vernacular used by respondents (Mariampolski, 1984). The importance of this cannot be overstressed, since successful promotional literature should address consumers using language and symbols they can and will interpret.

A fourth benefit of focus group interviews is that they permit the assessment of nonverbal responses. For example, body language, facial expressions, voice tone, and the physical handling of catalogues and brochures provide significant indicators about the way in which issues and materials are being perceived or used.

The drawbacks of focus group interviews include, first, the cost. Estimates of expenses range from $1,500 to $4,500 per discussion session, depending on the use and cost of outside service providers and incentives, difficulty of recruiting qualified respondents, and moderator costs. Travel and the staff time of observers may add significantly to this amount. A college or university that uses its own facilities and staff can substantially reduce costs.

A second drawback is the potential overenthusiasm over findings and a tendency to treat results as scientific and generalizable. The results of focus group studies should rarely be used alone; rather, they should be used in concert with findings from other types of research before expensive or irreversible decisions are made.

Third, recruiting appropriate respondents is more difficult than is immediately apparent. Consequently, it may be important to use an outside firm experienced at recruitment unless it is appropriate for a study to use accessible and easily identified participants such as currently enrolled students. Finally, some people are simply better able to express their ideas than others, and their comments may be given more credence or attention because they are more articulate.

Suggestions for Planning Focus Group Studies

Most of the crucial steps in planning and conducting a focus group study have been identified in this chapter. Clearly, successful studies require thoughtful planning, careful implementation, cautious analyses, and the judicious use of findings. Additional points to consider are these:

- Clarify the general approach and specific purpose of a study before it is conducted, and be sure that all relevant parties in the institution agree on or at least understand them.
- Obtain consensus about the one thing those commissioning the study would most like to learn.
- Limit the number of topics to be discussed so that each one can be given sufficient attention. Focus group interviews are best at

eliciting in-depth information about one or two issues rather than superficial information about many (Hollander and Oromaner, 1986).

• Recruit and screen respondents carefully.

• Understand the limitations of focus group interviews—they are not a replacement for quantitative research.

• Give the moderator ample time to analyze the results; do not expect a thoughtful analysis in the immediate stimulation and excitement of a discussion session (Roller, 1985).

• Limit the number of observers, have a researcher present who can explain focus group processes to them and maintain a non-party atmosphere, and debrief observers at the conclusion of a discussion session (Smith, 1986).

Conclusion

Focus group interviews can enable colleges and universities to understand their clientele, generate ideas for new and improved marketing programs, and evaluate the effectiveness of such programs. The insights gained from focus group interviews can prevent costly errors. Though their planning and implementation may appear casual and inexpensive, high-quality focus group studies require adherence to rigorous standards, skilled personnel, and adequate financial resources. Focus group interviewing is neither cheap nor easy, but when well done it is a powerful tool for market research and an important complement to quantitative studies.

References

Bers, T. H., and Smith-Bandy, K. "College Choice and the Non-Traditional Student." Paper presented at the Association for Institutional Research Annual Forum, Orlando, Florida, June 22–25, 1986.

Calder, B. J. "Focus Groups and the Nature of Qualitative Marketing Research." *Journal of Marketing Research*, 1977, *14*, 353–364.

Dickenson, S. B. "A Little 'Sensitizing' Is Helpful for Marketers." *Marketing News*, 1986, *20*, 50.

Fram, E. H. "How Focus Groups Unlock Market Intelligence: Tapping In-House Researchers." *Business Marketing*, 1985, *70*, 80–82.

Goldman, A. E., and McDonald, S. S. *The Group Depth Interview: Its Principles and Practices*. Englewood Cliffs, N.J.: Prentice-Hall, 1987.

Hess, J. M. "Group Interviewing." In R. L. King (ed.), *New Science of Planning*. Chicago: American Marketing Association, 1968.

Higgenbotham, J. B., and Cox, K. K. *Focus-Group Interviews: A Reader*. Chicago: American Marketing Association, 1979.

Hollander, S. L., and Oromaner, D. S. "Seminars Fill Gap in Focus-Group Training." *Marketing News*, 1986, *20*, 46.

Langer, J. Quoted in "Focus Groups Aid Search for New Markets." *Marketing News*, 1986, *20*, 54.

Mariampolski, H. "The Resurgence of Qualitative Research." *Public Relations Journal*, 1984, *40*, 21–23.

Roller, M. R. "Mental Image of Groups Is Out of Focus." *Marketing News*, 1985, *19*, 21, 26.

Smith, A. "Researchers Must Control Focus Group—and Those Behind the Mirror as Well." *Marketing News*, 1986, *20*, 33–35, 36.

Welch, J. L. "Researching Marketing Problems and Opportunities with Focus Groups." *Industrial Marketing Management*, 1985, *14*, 245–253.

Trudy H. Bers is senior director of institutional research, curriculum, and strategic planning at Oakton College, Des Plaines, Illinois. Among her primary responsibilities are the planning and implementation of market research studies for the college.

Marketing research offers a positive approach to program planning. A case study of Arapahoe Community College illustrates a range of techniques for gauging market potential.

Assessing the Market Potential for New Programs

Richard A. Voorhees

At a time when many institutions struggle to remain viable in the face of dwindling resources, it is ironic that most of the initiatives relating to instructional programs have been directed toward formal review leading to closure of some programs. For most public institutions fear of program discontinuation has generated great concern and has spurred time-consuming efforts to collect a wide variety of data which has resulted in less time and energy directed toward the pursuit of new or replacement programs. While program review provides a structure for scaling down and eliminating programs, a careful assessment of market opportunities holds the promise of strengthening institutional vitality. This chapter offers a framework for assessing the market potential for new programs.

Program–Market Opportunity Matrix

Kotler and Fox (1985) suggest that institutions begin to identify market potentials through use of a program–market opportunity matrix. This nine-cell matrix allows institutions to place present and future programs along two dimensions, markets (existing, geographical, new) and

R. S. Lay and J. J. Endo (eds.). *Designing and Using Market Research.*
New Directions for Institutional Research, no. 54. San Francisco: Jossey-Bass, Summer 1987.

programs (existing, modified, and new). This matrix forms the basis for the following terms associated with market potentials that are used in this chapter:

Existing Program Developments. This consists of deeper penetration of existing markets, geographical expansion, or finding new market segments for existing programs. This is what many institutions do under the rubric of "marketing"; that is, colleges increase their promotion of existing programs or search for new market segments for existing programs.

Program Modification. This occurs when institutions modify programs with either existing or new markets in mind. The natural tendency of most institutions when faced with enrollment shortfalls is to repackage existing courses and programs under different labels and offer them at different times and in varying formats in order to attract students. This process can promote short-term institutional survival but may not produce fundamental changes in programs necessary for long-term institutional health.

New Program Development. This refers to the process of creating new programs for existing, modified, or totally new markets. Total innovation occurs when an institution decides to create new classes, departments, or schools designed specifically for new markets. The creation of "universities without walls" during the 1960s and 1970s represents total innovation because of the focus on serving theretofore underserved populations of nontraditional students.

Points of Departure

Institutions embarking on the paths leading to program modification or new program development must ask a series of interrelated yet fundamental questions at the outset. First, what is the relationship between current programs and a proposed new program? New programs must be balanced with existing offerings to ensure that the new "mix" is compatible with existing structures. A new program usually requires a general education component that must be accommodated through "service" courses. A new program, particularly one planned for market segments with special needs, may also require new college services. Given a documented need, will college trustees, the administration, and the faculty be willing to add to or modify service classes and student services in order to accommodate new market segments?

Second, how does the proposed program match the needs of current students? A new program may attract a new type of student, resulting in a change in the composition of the student body. The opposite is true as well; a new program may appeal only to a narrow cross-section of current students and may fail to attract new students. The changes brought about because of program modification or innovation may be unsatisfactory to current students who may resent not only the new students themselves but also the changes that have occurred because of the new students. Introduction of new programs that are radically different from current institutional offerings is likely to interject a challenge to existing organizational culture. Introduction of a new, dissimilar program may be perceived as an affront by current students, faculty, alumni, and other important publics.

Third, what is the impact of the proposed program on institutional resources? Even if totally self-supporting in the short-term, campus constituencies may view new programs as diverting resources needed to maintain or expand existing programs. If a commitment has been made to preserve the status quo, an institution may be unable to afford new programs even in the best of circumstances.

Finally, how does the proposed program fit in with the institutional role and mission? Operating in a financially constrained environment, governing boards of the 1980s will hardly grant approval to new initiatives they do not perceive to be consonant with the institutional role and mission.

The search for answers to these questions is the starting point in any process of new program development. The techniques that follow can bring other questions into clearer focus.

Techniques to Assess the Market Potential for New Programs

Techniques used to develop instructional programs should be structured to answer two central questions: Is there a pool of prospective students who are likely to enroll? and what is the market for program graduates? Fortunately, a variety of publications easily available through most libraries can begin to address the answers to both questions.

First, the U.S. Census Bureau, in addition to the major census conducted every ten years, updates demographic information on a periodic basis. For institutions that draw students from regional or national markets, state summaries of census data may be aggregated. For institutions that serve an explicitly defined geographical area, census data are reported by more discrete units, termed census tracts, the boundaries of which are configured so that they contain an average of four thousand people.

Second, government and quasi-governmental agencies, such as regional governmental planning agencies, state labor departments, and legislative clearinghouses use census data to prepare reports on demographic and employment trends. Given a sufficient rationale, these agencies also can prepare reports customized to institutional specifications.

Third, chambers of commerce, banks, utility companies, and similar agencies and employers operating within a given geographical area generate reports that focus on demographic trends, employment data, and economic forecasts. Taken collectively or in combination these information sources can provide institutions with the basic data needed to begin addressing the question of where new students can be found and can serve as an indicator of employment opportunities for students enrolled in programs leading directly to careers. As a starting point, this "off the shelf" data can illuminate other potential questions necessary for program development.

Surveys of Prospective Students. Most institutions conduct surveys of potential employers; fewer institutions survey prospective students. The lack of information about prospective students is a significant shortcoming in assessing the market potential for new programs. At a minimum, surveys of prospective students seek to identify the demographic characteristics, educational aspirations, and current education levels of respondents. At the most, these studies also seek to determine preferences for specific types of instruction, scheduling choices, the extent to which information on existing programming reaches its intended audience, and perceptions of institutional image. In addition to profiling career-related preferences, surveys of this nature can also point to the desire to increase general knowledge in liberal arts areas.

A recent random survey of adults residing in Arapahoe Community College's service area in Colorado (Voorhees and Hart, 1985) has been instrumental in pointing to market potentials. The Arapahoe study found, among other adult educational preferences, that as the respondent's age increased, so did the perceived need for classes in the liberal arts. Also crucial to Arapahoe College's planning for off-campus classes and services was the finding that 77 percent of all adults surveyed indicated that they would not drive more than ten miles to attend college classes.

Surveys of Current Students. The opinions and aspirations of currently enrolled students and the insights they might offer about program development are often overlooked. Since these students are currently enrolled in one or more college classes, they are easily accessible and serve as a microcosm of the opinions of new students. It is reasonable to expect that the perceptions current students hold about institutional services such as job placement, parking, and child care may not differ significantly from those of new students. Perceptions of institutional image and the quality of campus life may, however, be expected to differ according to the socioeconomic background, previous educational experience, and age of prospective students.

Several commercially available instruments can be used to supplement an institution's efforts to capture student attitudes and opinions through "home-grown" instruments. These include the American College Testing Service's *Evaluation Survey Service* (ESS), the *Cooperative Institutional Research Program* (CIRP) surveys developed by the Higher Education Research Institute at the University of California at Los Angeles, and the *Student-Outcomes Information Service* (SOIS) surveys developed by the National Center for Higher Education Management Systems and the College Entrance Examination Board. In addition to providing information about current students' opinions and attitudes that are specific to a given campus, each of these survey services can provide normative data that researchers can use to compare student demographic characteristics, attitudes, and opinions about the campus with national profiles.

Values and Lifestyles (VALS). The VALS typology (Thomas, 1981), developed by Scientific Research Institute International, divides Americans into nine consumer types identified by lifestyle (Table 1). These types, or psychographic profiles, are grouped into four lifestyle categories on the basis of attitudes, consumption patterns, and demographics.

Until the 1970s, market research in the private sector was dominated by demographic segmentation, that is, the classification of potential consumers by age, income, level of education, and other quantitative variables. The emergence of the baby boomers, whose consumer habits were radically different from previous generations, and the disappearance of the captive housewife, as more women entered the workforce, contributed to the demise of demographic research; people were no longer behaving or consuming products in ways that traditional research could explain.

The VALS typology can be used to match proposals for new program with appropriate audiences, and it is particularly helpful for institutions looking for fresh ways to consider the needs and attitudes of new adult markets. VALS research, for instance, suggests that "outer-directed" people are more likely to consume a product or participate in an activity if it is perceived to be popular. In contrast, "inner-directed" people appear to need reassurance that they have the capabilities needed to accomplish a particular task or activity. It appears that "survivors," because of their lack of higher education and despairing attitudes, would be the most difficult group to match with new programs. Alternatively, "societally conscious" people have usually completed a college education but come back to the college classroom to further their interests in the arts. Obviously, the scheduling options, delivery mechanisms, and even program content designed for these groups would need to be signficantly different.

Employment Surveys and Studies. Table 2 shows the most frequently used types of surveys and studies for determining the marketability of career program graduates. Among these techniques, the employer survey, in which employers are asked to estimate their future need for trained personnel, is the most popular. Employer surveys are used most often in local markets because the proximity of employers to the institution ensures a higher rate of return. Properly conducted, these surveys can be the first step in involving employers in program development. Employer estimates of personnel requirements, however, often suffer from reliability and validity problems. This is especially true among smaller employers who often lack the expertise to anticipate future technological developments that may affect their position within a given employment field.

Less frequent among employment surveys and studies are econometric studies in which an array of input variables is used to model job demand by occupational categories over a ten-year period. These studies, produced by the Bureau of Labor Statistics, are perhaps more reliable and valid than institutionally produced employer studies. However, they are

Table 1. The VALS Typology

Lifestyle Category	Percent of Population	Lifestyle Type	Demographic Characteristics	Attitudes
Need-Driven	11	Survivors	Over 55; no college; retired; $10,000 average income; 73 percent female	Despairing; conservative; resigned
		Sustainers	Under 30; ethnic; unemployed; under $15,000 median income	Hopeful; resentful; unconcerned with rules
Inner-Directed	19	I-Am-Me's	Under 30; single; college students; low to middle income	Spontaneous; receptive to new ideas, situations, and environments
		Experientials	Under 30; college-educated; unmarried; $26,000 median income	Idealistic; emotional; liberal
		Societally Conscious	Mid-thirties; college educated; professionals; $32,000 median income	Self-reliant; socially responsible; strong interest in the arts
Outer-Directed	68	Belongers	Mid-fifties; $15,000 median income; small towns; clerks and housewives	Conforming; unexperimental; family- and home-oriented
		Emulators	Under 30; urban dwellers; low education, $20,000 median income; salesworkers, crafts workers	Ambitious; frustrated; envious
		Achievers	Middle-aged; primarily male; married; some college; $35,000 median income	Decisive; competitive; in search of fame and material success
Integrated	2		Well-educated; professionals and executives; married; $34,000+ income	Extremely self-aware; trusting; supportive of free enterprise

Source: Atlas, 1984.

built on assumptions that forecast productivity, consumption, and overall economic output, each of which may be expected to vary widely, or at least unpredictably, over the course of ten years.

Forecasting technological change or economic trends is at best a risky business. For this reason, many organizations have turned to environmental scanning as a strategic planning technique. Environmental scanning can provide decision makers with information on the latest developments in key issues related to organizational survival, including unfolding trends in technology, employment rates, relocation of major industries, productivity rates, and consumer patterns. One can easily see how environmental scanning can inform all phases of program development, in general, and econometric studies, trend extrapolation research, and job vacancy studies, in particular.

Program Need Index. For schools operating in geographical areas where more than one institution produces graduates in a given field, the Program Need Index (PNI) suggested by Nielsen (1981) may be a useful technique for assessing the feasibility of initiating a new program. Used cautiously, the PNI allows an institution to compare the relative strength of current and proposed programs in a geographically defined labor market while accounting for the presence or absence of similar programs offered at competing institutions. The PNI is given by the following formula:

$$\text{Index} = \frac{\text{Number of current employees in targeted employment area}}{\text{Number of graduates in area with related majors}}$$

At a minimum, the value computed for the PNI should exceed one. Values lower than one indicate that there are more programs producing graduates in a given geographical area than the labor market can absorb. To illustrate how PNI analyses work, I offer the following hypothetical examples for a geographical area in which a number of petroleum engineers are employed:

Example of the PNI for a master's degree program in petroleum engineering:

$$\frac{5,000 \text{ people employed as engineers in area}}{250 \text{ graduating master's degree engineers from area colleges}} = 20$$

Example for an undergraduate petroleum engineering program:

$$\frac{5,000 \text{ people employed as engineers in area}}{1,000 \text{ graduating bachelor's degree engineers from area schools}} = 5$$

Table 2. Employment Surveys and Study Techniques for Program Development

Type	Purpose	Advantages	Disadvantages
Industry Survey	Determines all possible jobs within a given industry; points to all related jobs such as field workers, accountants, engineers, trainers, secretaries, and others	Provides a picture of the entire strata of jobs	Must be very complete to show need for related occupations
Job Survey	Determines whether and what programs are needed in a single occupation	Points to specific occupational needs; preliminary to curriculum development	Focuses on only one occupation; must survey across many employment settings
Employer Survey	Determines local or regional employment needs; more in-depth than occupations survey because employers are asked to project needs	Provides trends; involves employers in planning	Projections may lack reliability and validity
Econometric Studies	Conducted by the Bureau of Labor Statistics, U.S. Department of Labor, to determine ten-year employment needs based on population, labor force, productivity, consumption, and overall output; estimates openings by occupation	More reliable than employer surveys; sophisticated methodology	Statistics are national, not always useful for regional or local projections; predictability based on economic forecasts for ten-year period
Job Vacancy Studies	Combines econometric studies with local or regional data to analyze present employment needs	Customizes data for regional purposes	Deals only with present needs; does not predict future needs

Trend Extra-polation Studies	Forecasts trends on basis of past trends	Inexpensive; quickly accomplished	Does not account for rapid change in the labor market; useful only for very short-term predictions
Environmental Scanning	Ongoing search for select information from a wide variety of sources to inform program development	Can provide the latest information on economic trends, labor markets, and political climates	Time consuming; can be expensive; care must be taken to ensure that proper categories for program development are scanned

In these examples the index value for the graduate petroleum engineering program is twenty, while the value for the undergraduate program is five, suggesting that the competitive position for the graduate degree program is considerably better. However, before resources are shifted to support the graduate program as a result of these formulas, more research is desirable. Perhaps further research would indicate that baccalaureate-level training in petroleum engineering is sufficient for entry into the field and that a graduate degree is superfluous for entrance.

Obviously, it would be unwise to accept the results of the PNI applied to an institution's programs without first realizing its limitations. In the foregoing examples we would first have to carefully determine what percentage of available jobs were accessible to candidates with a graduate degree before we could entertain weighty decisions about where to direct institutional resources. Data-driven techniques such as the PNI are also more difficult to apply to liberal arts programs for the simple reason that relevant data are scarce. To be relevant for a given institution, more information, primarily student follow-up data, is needed to determine what percentages of liberal arts graduates enter graduate school, find immediate employment, or elect to pursue studies in other fields. For those students electing to extend their educations, institutions will want to know the types of subjects they are studying. Similarly, for those graduates who elect to work, institutions should know which employment fields they enter. More knowledge of the postgraduation experiences of all graduates, particularly those of liberal arts students, can point the way to the modification of existing curricula or the need for new program development.

External Advisory Committees. External advisory committees are more common among two-year institutions. These groups, consisting of qualified professionals from the field that the new program is intended to address, can be invaluable in determining whether a new instructional program will be successful. Representatives from the private sector can act as a sounding board for employment needs and can provide priceless insights into the curricular content of a proposed program. Formed on a standing basis to assist institutional decision makers, program advisory committees, when properly constructed with an eye to wide representation of employers within a specific employment market, can save the college from making false starts in launching new programs and can confirm or dispel data that an institution has collected to support program development. Later, after the program is launched, program advisory committees can suggest benchmarks for program evaluation and can provide program graduates with valuable employment leads.

Program Creation: A Case Study

At Arapahoe Community College (ACC), ten new instructional programs have been created over the past five years. The majority of these programs have been conceived by faculty members, and each has been subject to ACC's guidelines for new program development and a subsequent process of external review at the state level. No new program is implemented at ACC if it cannot be demonstrated that at least 50 percent of all graduates can be employed in jobs directly related to their education and that they will earn a reasonable return on their educational investment. To illustrate several of the techniques discussed earlier, we turn to a program developed during the 1984–1985 academic year and initiated at ACC the following summer. On the surface, this example may appear only to apply to two-year colleges. The techniques that are illustrated, the use of program advisory committees and the PNI, can easily be extended to assess the market potential for career programs at four-year colleges and universities.

Arapahoe County, Colorado, is the seventh fastest-growing county in the United States. Concomitant with this unprecedented growth is the need for expanded public services, including the need for a new detention facility. As is the case with other local governments in the 1980s, Arapahoe County could identify resources to build a new detention facility, but could not identify a cost-effective means of training the professional personnel required to operate it.

For more than four years, ACC has operated an instructional program to certify police officers. Completion of this program, entitled the Basic Police Academy, leads to state certification. Instructors in the Basic Police Academy assist students in job placement and conduct routine follow-up on graduates' job performance. This program, as mandated by ACC's governing board, also maintains an advisory committee consisting of representatives from law enforcement agencies, which meets a minimum of twice a year.

When plans to construct the new Arapahoe County detention facility became public, the faculty members operating the police academy and advisory committee members quickly saw an opportunity to develop a new program that would draw on existing expertise. The county announced that it would need to hire two hundred additional officers by the time the new facility opened. Contact was quickly made with officials in the county sheriff's office to determine the starting salaries for these new officers and to explore plans for a detention officer's academy based on ACC's successful Basic Police Academy. Starting salaries for new officers were established at $1,700 per month, satisfying ACC's criterion to develop programs in which graduates could expect to earn a reasonable return on their investment. Based on the reputation of the Basic Police Academy as advanced by advisory committee members, county law enforcement officials were interested in working with ACC and expressed an interest in hiring all program graduates.

Two research questions were posed at this point in the process: Would enrollment be sufficient to cover instructional salaries, administrative overhead, and other costs associated with this new program? and Would succeeding graduating classes also be able to find employment? (or Would the demand for detention officers be satisfied after one or two classes had graduated?) Since starting salaries were very high for positions requiring only ten weeks of training, the answer to the first question then depended on the extent to which qualified applicants could be admitted. Here, the existing network established through the Basic Police Academy was of crucial importance in identifying prospective students. ACC officials also wrote a successful grant request to train detention officers, which provided instructional costs for one year. A combination of promotion by ACC, contact with prospective students by advisory committee members and faculty, and grant resources provided a positive answer to the first question.

To determine whether succeeding graduating classes could also find employment, contact was made with four other metropolitan area county sheriff's departments and the Colorado State Department of Labor and Employment. Since two of the four counties were in different stages of constructing new detention facilities and the other counties were considering similar construction, each expressed keen interest in the program. The high turnover associated with work as a detention officer (about 40 percent annually), together with the need for program graduates in the metropolitan Denver area (based on construction of three new facilities, two hundred officers would be needed annually for three years and a constant 120 would be needed annually thereafter), would provide a sufficiently high projection to sustain the program in succeeding years. While it is probably not practical to forecast any employment need across long periods of time, the Department of Labor and Employment confirmed ACC's conclusion that the state had a shortage of prison space and that new prisons and detention personnel were likely to be a pressing priority throughout the 1990s. Given the fact that ACC does not compete with other institutions within the state in training detention officers, data for the following Program Need Index analysis were easily collected:

An example of short-term (three-year) PNI analysis for the metropolitan area:

$$\frac{600 \text{ detention officers needed in the metropolitan area}}{200 \text{ graduating from ACC's Detention Officer's Academy}} = 3$$

An example of short-term (three-year) PNI analysis for the state:

$$\frac{900 \text{ detention officers needed statewide}}{200 \text{ graduating from ACC's Detention Officer's Academy}} = 4.5$$

Each of these values exceeds one. Given a lack of competition from other institutions, the PNI indicates that the market would appear to absorb as many graduates as ACC could produce.

Conclusion

The time is ripe for institutional research personnel to increase their involvement in instructional programming beyond the role required for program review and discontinuation. This chapter has presented techniques to assess the market potential for new programs, which institutional researchers can utilize to increase their involvement in this crucial component of institutional survival.

The bulk of program development in the higher education enterprise during the past ten years has been in programs that prepare students for vocations and careers. Accordingly, the most frequently used techniques focus on employers and employment needs. The advantages and disadvantages of seven specific employer surveys and study techniques have been presented in this chapter. The most popular of these techniques, the employer survey, promotes employer involvement in program development but may also lack validity and reliability. Other employment-related study techniques are more sophisticated but may be insensitive to rapid changes in labor markets.

Surveys of current students can produce invaluable insights for assessing market potentials. Among the information institutions should collect from these surveys are preferences for scheduling options, delivery mechanisms, perceptions of existing college services, and preferences for specific programs. Several commercially available surveys—including the ESS, CIRP, and SOIS surveys—can provide researchers with a convenient means of comparing marketing information for currently enrolled students with national profiles. These data can point to needed information on *existing* programs and services, which can illuminate the processes of new program development. While more difficult to obtain, similar data should also be collected for new target markets. As institutions expand into new markets, the preferences of prospective students for scheduling, program content, and institutional services must match the institution's ability to deliver.

Among the newer techniques reviewed in this chapter are Values and Lifestyles research and the Program Need Index. These techniques provide new ways of approaching the fit between proposed programs and the market need for new and existing programs, respectively. The VALS typology, in particular, represents a departure from traditional demographic market research and presents a fresh framework for matching programs with student characteristics.

Interest in program development appears to be on the rise as more institutions realize that their very survival is at stake. This trend calls for an activist role for institutional research offices. During the initiation and pre-implementation phases of program development, institutional personnel should forge alliances with personnel responsible for student recruitment, alterations in curricula, delivery systems, and student services. After new programs are implemented, immediate ties to other functional campus units can help the institutional research office evaluate the success of new programs.

For the foreseeable future, public institutions will continue to face external pressures to eliminate nonproductive programs. This, in tandem with increased competition among institutions for students, provides an agenda that might appear to undercut institutional vitality. Against this backdrop, the techniques to assess the market potential for new programs presented here merit consideration at many institutions.

References

Atlas, J. "Beyond Demographics." *Atlantic*, 1984, *254*, 49–58.

Kotler, P., and Fox, K.F.A. *Strategic Marketing for Educational Institutions*. Englewood Cliffs, N.J.: Prentice-Hall, 1985.

Nielsen, R. P. "Evaluating Market Opportunities for Academic Programs with a Program—Employment Opportunities—Competing Institutions Index." *College and University*, 1981, *56*, 178–182.

Thomas, T. C. *Values and Lifestyles: The New Psychographics?* Paper presented at the Advertising Research Foundation conference, New York, February 24, 1981.

Voorhees, R. A., and Hart, S. *An Analysis of the Educational Preferences Among Adult Residents of Arapahoe Community College's Service Area*. Littleton, Colo.: Arapahoe Community College, 1985. (ED 266 835)

Richard A. Voorhees is associate vice-president for instruction at Arapahoe Community College in Littleton, Colorado, where he is responsible for marketing, planning, and research.

Institutional planners responsible for setting enrollment
objectives and levels must develop an understanding of college
market structure, choose among alternate approaches to market
assessment, and apply appropriate methods for measuring
patterns of competition.

Describing Patterns of Competition

Glenwood L. Rowse

Market stuctures define the competitive environment within which prospective students choose colleges. Because colleges typically draw students from overlapping pools of applicants, they are in competition even though they may not be consciously competing or even aware of the overlap in student interests. Consequently, the fortunes of an institution may depend as much or more on events affecting other institutions and student pools than on its own actions. A rippling effect may occur, with events originating in different types of colleges, quite quickly altering the competitive position of one's own college. Thus, it is important for each institution to understand not only its immediate competitors but the broader set of competitive groups and how they are related as well.

How should the institutional research proceed? A thorough analysis of market structures is a highly demanding time-consuming activity. Glover (1986) describes management information that can be gathered and analyzed, ranging from assessing population or client trends to performing college similarity studies, to conducting accepted applicant surveys. Available data sources range from published population and college data and projections to services such as the enrollment planning service of the College Entrance Examination Board (CEEB), to annual freshmen surveys, to institutionally conducted surveys. All of these activities are useful, but the

R. S. Lay and J. J. Endo (eds.). *Designing and Using Market Research.*
New Directions for Institutional Research, no. 54. San Francisco: Jossey-Bass, Summer 1987.

data sets all have important limitations. Ideally, a college needs a data set specific to its own competition, covering all relevant variables and stages of the college choice process. Applicant surveys are feasible as institutional surveys, but they cover a restricted market and typically have very low response rates. A means must be found to both provide a comprehensive data set and ease the skill and time burdens of what is a very difficult and complex research task.

Perhaps a solution lies in the development of external services similar in concept to the CEEB enrollment planning service. Through the use of new or upgraded existing surveys (for example, current population surveys or high school and beyond longitudinal surveys) better data sets should be developed for a variety of market segments. To fully assess competition, data must be available for those considering work, military, delayed attendance, or other options as well as those applying to primary college competitors. Data must also include detailed student and college characteristics. Typically, sample sizes must be large to deal with the "rare event" nature of college preference data and the wide geographical draw of many colleges. Partial summarization of this data and general consulting by professional staff prior to detailed analysis at individual colleges would provide a valuable support structure. Such a service might be developed by private organizations, state agencies, or consortiums of colleges. Surveys would then be more professionally developed, and response rates higher because the single questionnaire for several colleges would have greater legitimacy. In one recent effort to survey all high school seniors in an area, high school counselors found such a survey useful for their own purposes and were highly cooperative. Regardless of the general strategy adopted for obtaining information and analyzing market structures, institutional researchers need to ask the right questions, understand alternative methods, and be aware of important issues in measuring competition. The following sections provide a conceptual framework, describe an "interest overlap" approach to assessing market structure, and discuss specific measures of competition and issues of variable selection.

A Conceptual Framework—Questions to Answer

Institutional planners should be able to describe several aspects of their own markets and competitive structures. In general, this involves identifying who competes with whom for which clientele under existing and anticipated conditions. More specifically, institutional researchers should seek to develop information related to all of the following questions:
Who is the competition?
- What are the numbers and sizes of competing institutions?
- What degree of competition exists—how much overlap in student interests exists both within and across competitive institutions?

- Are competing institutions highly similar or distinctive?
- Is it reasonable for an institution to focus on a few key competitors, or is the broader competitive structure crucial?
- To what extent is there competition with noncollege options as well as with other colleges?

Who are the clients?

- Which student characteristics are most useful in explaining competitive advantages and differences?
- To what extent does an institution and each of its competitors serve a relatively homogeneous client group or seek to balance the desires of a diverse clientele?
- To what extent is each group of prospective students firmly set in their college preferences or able to be swayed—that is, susceptible to recruitment activities?

What dynamics and conditions are strategic for planning?

- Do clear dominance patterns exist within and across groups of competing institutions?
- Are the competitive groups and dominance patterns stable or volatile?
- Can shifts in competitive position be anticipated given expected shifts in client population and interests as well as likely competitive actions taken by colleges?
- Are market structures and key policy levers different for different stages of the college choice and recruitment process?

Researchers have provided considerable understanding of the process by which a student selects a college and when and in what way each variable is influential. A useful summary is found in Jackson's (1980) description of three hypothetical phases in the process of selecting a college. They are the development of college aspirations and general preferences, exclusion of clearly inappropriate alternatives, and evaluation of the remaining alternatives. Since measurement usually occurs near the time of selection of a college, Jackson assumes that preference is probably constrained for those students from low-income and otherwise limiting backgrounds. He concludes that the strongest influences on college aspirations are academic achievement, social context, and family background, in that order.

In the phase during which colleges are being excluded, Jackson reports that college location, the available information about colleges, and major college characteristics exert the strongest influences. By the spring preceding high school graduation, most college-bound students have narrowed their attention to a small, choice set. The evaluation of that choice set results in the expected school of attendance. Because the evaluation process is typically between colleges having either small or subtle differences, Jackson believes that net cost differences are a major influence.

Also, because of the perception of few clear distinctions among colleges, student choices may be stochastic and not totally predictable. Prediction may be much more successful for types of colleges and students than for individual colleges and students. Another factor contributing to unpredictability and one not considered in Jackson's discussion is the control exerted by colleges in the admissions process through the number of available slots offered to students of various types each year and, in general, by the nature and quality of recruiting experienced by students (Chapman, 1981; Litten, 1982).

A General Approach to Assessing Market Structure

A particularly productive approach is offered by viewing "systems" of competing institutions. The most notable systems research studies are those by Zemsky and Oedel (1983), Rowse (1985), Rowse and Wing (1982), and Sullivan, Litten, Morris, and Brodigan (1980). The general steps present in all of these studies are (1) definition or identification of competitive college groups, (2) assessment of the degree of competition, and (3) analysis of college characteristics both within and across competitive groups. In all of these studies, overlap in college interest by the applicant pool served as the data to be analyzed. A brief look at several of these studies illustrates issues involved in analyzing student overlap data.

Zemsky and Oedel (1983) describe competition among types of colleges using a typology in common use. Overlap in Scholastic Aptitude Test (SAT) score submission requests for these college categories was measured in addition to several characteristics of students (in particular, distance from home to the college receiving the test scores). Table 1 provides the resulting overlap matrix for students in New England states who are interested in regional or national markets. Zemsky and Oedel concluded that students were frequently interested in a single type of college but that it was also not unusual for the boundaries to be crossed.

Average degree aspiration, parental education, SAT ability, and family income were found to increase for colleges ordered as follows: from public four-year colleges to in-state public flagships, to private linking and standard colleges and out-of-state public flagships, to private selective colleges, and, finally, to private flagships. The private standard colleges were notable for having considerable overlap with all other groups and perhaps being vulnerable based on both prestige or selectivity and price.

These general patterns are not sufficient for fully understanding competitive structures. In particular, the appropriate measure of overlap may depend on how various levels of overlap translate into firmness of preference. Also, it may be necessary to focus on the students bordering on making a different college choice, rather than on the general patterns. Shifts in enrollments may be determined more by how many students can

Table 1. Overlap in Test Score Submission Requests by Type of Institution

	Private Flagship	Private Selective	Private Standard	Private Linking	Out-of-State (OOS) Public Flagship	In-State (INS) Public Flagship	Four-Year Public
Number:							
Private Flagship	16,067						
Private Selective	11,416	25,999					
Private Standard	7,106	14,564	42,149				
Private Linking	5,487	9,646	13,999	24,956			
OOS Public Flagship	5,347	8,771	11,689	7,139	21,399		
INS Public Flagship	5,068	9,128	15,484	9,713	9,462	31,403	
Four-Year Public	3,602	6,201	17,250	10,662	8,571	14,676	36,763

Source: Zemsky and Oedel, 1983, p. 67.

be induced to cross the boundaries than by the general patterns. Existing overlap seems easily large enough to accommodate substantial shifts in enrollment. More detailed descriptions are needed to discover what might initiate a shift. Finally, these data reflect only one relatively late stage in the student choice process and one set of environmental conditions and college options.

Zemsky and Oedel (1983) predefined college groups and then used data to measure competition among them, while Rowse and Wing (1982) used data to describe empirical groupings of competitors. A large sample of freshmen in New York state was surveyed to identify those colleges that students considered attending prior to enrollment. Factor analysis was performed to identify groups of colleges from students' listings of colleges according to interest or application. By this technique, competitive groups were found to include from two to eight colleges, with most having four or five members. In the interest analysis, 151 colleges formed 36 groups. In the application analysis, 136 colleges formed 34 groups. This is approximately double the number of categories found in common institutional typologies, and it excludes several colleges that did not fit into a category with another college. Geographical proximity accounted for only a portion of the increased number of groups. No college listed more than seventy times failed to group with at least one other college; thus, it is suspected that factor analysis will identify only major groups of competitors and therefore poorly describe the competitive structure for smaller or programmatically distinct institutions. Other findings of structural characteristics were also suggested by this study: First, interest-derived groups were clearly different from application-derived groups and usually not clearly linked. Interest groups were more apt to be geographically related and were more apt to include a few colleges of clearly high reputation. Second, correlations between college and student characteristic variables tended to be stronger within rather than across competitive groups. Thus, differences on descriptive variables (especially SAT scores) within a group may reliably predict dominance patterns or preference hierarchies. "Crossover" colleges, which were of a different general type than others in a group, occurred frequently enough that reliance on standard college types appears inadequate.

A study of the preferences and expectations of eleven thousand New York state high school seniors in 1981 (Rowse, 1985) duplicated many of the findings of the earlier freshmen survey. However, several of the analyses also led to hypotheses that competitive groups are more complex and interrelated than was apparent from earlier studies. While the major competitive groups tended to stand out from all analyses, the specifics of their membership and linkages with others may be both more interrelated and transient than has been previously suggested. It also appears that the specific groups identified and their characteristics are sensitive to the specific methods used to identify them. Given the complexity of colleges and the diverse subpopulations that colleges may serve, it appears that great care in method selection combined with multiple analyses for various levels of detail and market segments may be necessary to adequately understand a college's competitive position. Specific considerations are described in the following sections.

Alternative Methods

The preceding section alluded to many of the analytical choices to be made by institutional researchers. The more significant choices are summarized in this section.

Conceptual or Data-Derived College Groups. Research indicates that conceptually similar types of colleges do not always correspond with data-derived competitive groups. The latter is the preferred method for enrollment planners at individual colleges. The tradeoff, however, is that the use of standard institutional categories gives the researcher access to comprehensive data bases such as those provided by the National Center for Education Statistics and the Census Bureau.

College Similarity or Client Interest. Data-derived college groups may be identified by clustering colleges with similar characteristics or by recording which colleges students say they are comparing. Groups based on stages of student interest (corresponding to the recruitment process) should be more precise and useful for planning purposes. Similarity analysis may be useful for assessing competitive position within groups identified in other ways. Comparisons may be directed to key determinants of choice for specific competitive college groups and subpopulations of students. Identification of those key variables is complex and may involve sophisticated multivariate analysis, educated judgment, and data exploration using techniques such as automatic interaction detection (see Chapter Seven).

Market Segmentation. Although colleges may be thought to have a general image and a typical student, the diversity within most colleges is nearly always great. For either conceptual or data-derived college groups, focusing on specific subpopulations permits more efficient design of recruitment strategies and much clearer images of competitive college groups. In fact, statistical methods for grouping colleges are weakened when the preferences entered for analysis come from a diverse set of students. Such an analysis may be expected to produce a small set of primary competitors consistent with general images. In the process, few student variables are likely to be associated with the competitive group, and key competitors for specific subpopulations of the college may not be identified.

Separate analyses may be useful for different age groups, ability groups, income groups, program-interest groups, cultural and social groups, and so on. College planners should not underestimate the capability of subpopulations of "fringe" clientele to produce large changes in the college's enrollment. Failure to attend to the concerns of and competitive events relevant to two or three subpopulations representing 30 percent of all enrollment could seriously alter the character and viability of the college. Similarly, manipulating admission levers to maintain enrollment levels during a period of decreasing applicant pools tends to affect disproportionately specific subpopulations. The result may be an important shift in the composition of students and the relevant set of college competitors (Wing and Rowse, 1986).

Stage of Competiton. Studies should be focused not only on specific subpopulations but also on specific stages in the college choice process. The tendency to focus on overlap in student applications may be reactive and place attention exclusively on student concerns about meeting college costs. Competitive groups obtained earlier in a student's selection process may be more important for positioning the institution to maximum advantage. Identifying an interest-based college group and improving one's own competitive position within that group may actually reduce applications sent to one's competitors, and thus lower the expense of competing on the basis of net cost alone.

Measuring Competition

Quantitative measures are needed to (1) group the colleges, (2) compare colleges within a competitive group, and (3) assess the relationship between colleges, college characteristics, and prospective student characteristics. Measures must effectively analyze rare events, categorical data, complex entities (colleges), and complex nonlinear relationships. Traditional methods of multivariate analysis may be inadequate because they are designed primarily for common events and linear relationships among variables measured using a continuous scale. However, interest in a specific college is inherently rare and categorical. College preference is complex and cannot be easily ordered on a few dimensions. In addition, complex interactions are increasingly being found to explain choice of college (Rowse, 1985). Measures must be selected that are appropriate for these conditions.

Product-moment correlations are the basis of traditional correlational methods. They were designed to measure linear covariation between two normally distributed continuous variables. To the extent that relationships are not linear or that two variables are not both normally distributed, the association may be seriously underestimated. In addition, a product-moment correlation makes an "omnibus type," covariance statement about the relationships between all levels of two variables (Reynolds, 1977). It is possible and common for two specific levels of two variables to generally co-occur while no notable relationship occurs for other levels of the two variables. To be able to identify these category-specific similarity patterns requires a different measure. Thus, the use of association measures for categorical variables would be of interest even if all data involved normally distributed continuous variables. The presence of many categorical variables such as individual colleges, college types, race or ethnicity, program interest, and the like only reinforces this need.

"Phi" is the most commonly used binary measure in traditional multivariate analysis. However, it is not a category-specific measure. A desirable measure would assess the degree to which categorical events co-occur at frequencies greater than would be expected from random distribution of the events. Few events are truly random, but it seems reasonable to expect that very idiosyncratic decisions produce a notable portion of the applications overlap between colleges. Overlap above and beyond statistically random overlap should reflect reliable competition between colleges due to their major characteristics. It is this portion of the applicants that may be most responsive to competitive actions taken by the paired colleges.

Category-specific associations are influenced both by the rarity of each categorical variable in the population under study and by the difference in the rarity of the paired variables. For example, assume that of all high school graduates expecting to attend college the fall after graduation, 200 applied to two or more multiple campus universities (multiversities). Also assume that 1,000 of 6,000 graduates may be classified as high-ability and that 150 of the 1,000 applied to two or more multiversities, as Table 2 illustrates.

The degree of association, as measured by phi, is 0.29. This is usually thought of as low-association, yet 75 percent of those applying to multiversities were high-ability students. Random application patterns would have resulted in only 33 applications to multiversities by high-ability graduate (200*1000/6000), far fewer than the 150 observed. Even if all 200 high-ability graduates had applied to multiversities, phi would be only 0.415. These low phi values are due first to the disparity in category frequencies (multiversity = high-ability = 1000/200=5) and further lowered by the rarity of both events (multiversity = 200/6000 = 0.333 and high-ability = 1000/6000 = 0.167).

Table 2. Hypothetical Crossclassification of Two Events

		Event I: High Ability		
		Yes	No	
Event II:	Yes	150	50	200
Multiversity	No	850	4,950	5,800
		1,000	5,000	6,000

We might choose to interpret the 0.29 association as a notable association, and this would work well if all paired variables in the analysis had similar sample frequencies. However, we can expect that studies will include both common and rare events, similar to highly disparate sample frequencies. Males and females are evenly present in the population, while high-ability constitutes only 5 to 10 percent of the population. College attendance is a choice made by approximately 60 percent of the high school graduates, community college by 30 percent of those going to college, multiversity by 3 percent, and College "X" by 0.4 percent or less. When examining the overlap in applications between two colleges of different sizes, it would be common with a large sample to find 50 applicants to the smaller college and 300 to a large competing college. The disparity between these frequencies is 6:1. The maximum possible phi that could be observed is approximately 0.04. Yet if most of the applicants to the smaller college are also applying to the larger college, a competitive situation of importance to the smaller college certainly exists.

To deal with these concerns, measures other than the phi are available. Within the context of correlation methods, Muthen (1984) has made considerable effort to use alternative measures and to adapt methods for them. The odds ratio used for log-linear analysis also appears to be a useful alternative to phi (Fleiss, 1981). Another option is a category interspecific association measure proposed and used extensively by Rowse (1985) as a statistic for categorical factor analysis. This statistic is called COLES (Categorical Observed Less Expected Scaled.) An essentially equivalent measure was discussed by Bimini in 1898 (see Goodman and Kruskal, 1979) and by Cole (1949).

COLES is the observed overlap between two colleges minus the expected overlap from random co-occurrences divided by the maximum possible overlap beyond random co-occurrences. Statistically, this measure is equivalent to phi over phi-max (or phi-min for negative associations), but it is not subject to concerns found in the literature regarding phi over phi-max if one's purpose is the measurement of category interspecific association rather than overall relationship between two continuums. The COLES association of multiversity with high-ability is 0.70 (compared to phi = 0.29). If all students applying to multiversities were high-ability, COLES would equal 1.0. The use of measures that adjust for statistically random overlap produce quite different results from those produced by other measures.

Zemsky and Oedel (1983) measured the extent of overlap between colleges simply by using co-applications as a percentage of the smaller number of applications received by either college for any given pair. A maximum overlap of 42 percent was assumed to reflect a substantial association. Table 3 replicates Zemsky and Oedel's overlap data for test score submissions, and Figure 1 adds COLES for comparison purposes. Of twenty-one possible pairings between the seven types of colleges reported on in that study, ten pairs produced a maximum percent overlap of 42 percent or higher. Several other pairs produced overlap measures close to the 42 percent criterion. The selection of cutoffs for overlap measures is always difficult and should be approached cautiously. Seven pairs produced a COLES of 0.10 or higher. The fewer strong associations observed by using COLES suggests greater distinctiveness and less competition between these college types. This may be true or the finding may be an artifact of using total overlap data to calculate associations for complex entities such as colleges.

As shown in Table 3, the competitive structure identified by Zemsky and Oedel was a highly interrelated structure. After ordering college types vertically based on average SAT scores, almost every college type was linked with another type both above and below on the scale. Private standard colleges appear to occupy a central position in the structure. However, based on COLES, private standard colleges appear not to be central. They grouped only with the private linking and private selective college types at levels above random overlap. The large number of private standard colleges produced by far the largest number of test score submissions and consequently the largest expected random overlap with other colleges.

The COLES structure also suggests that there may be two distinct private sector groupings with most public and private sector competition occurring between the public out-of-state flagship colleges and the private flagship and selective colleges. Four-year public colleges appear to be competitively isolated based on COLES, rather than being feeders to other public and private colleges as suggested by maximum percent overlap. This finding is reinforced by examining strong negative COLES associations.

Figure 1. Structural Linkages Among Institutions

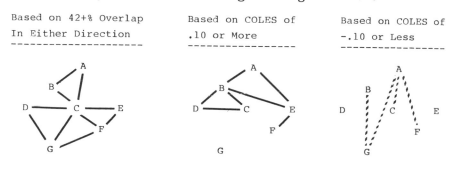

Based on 42+% Overlap In Either Direction

Based on COLES of .10 or More

Based on COLES of -.10 or Less

Note: COLES was calculated using an *N* of 84,036 students.

Table 3. Percent of Overlap in Test Score Submissions

	Private Flagship	Private Selective	Private Standard	Private Linking	Out-of-State (OOS) Public Flagship	In-State (INS) Public Flagship	Four-Year Public
Private Flagship	—	.58	-.12	.06	.10	-.15	-.49
Private Selective	71%	—	.12	.11	.15	-.06	-.46
Private Standard	44%	56%	—	.12	.09	-.02	-.06
Private Linking	34%	39%	56%	—	.05	.02	-.02
Out-Of-State Public Flagship	33%	41%	55%	33%	—	.11	-.08
In-State Public Flagship	32%	35%	49%	39%	44%	—	.05
Four-Year Public	22%	24%	47%	43%	40%	47%	—

Source: Zemsky and Oedel, 1983, p. 67.

As might have been expected, public four-year colleges overlapped with private flagship and selective colleges at levels below random expected overlap. However, they also linked negatively with private linking colleges and public in-state flagships. Given current perceptions, the public four-year colleges do not appear to be a strong source of students for the private sector in a period of enrollment decline. The popular conception that many private standard and linking colleges are vulnerable in a period of demographic decline is supported by the lack of an overlap between these colleges and public (or lower-SAT colleges) in the COLES structure. Some relief might be felt by those in private standard colleges in that a strong negative COLES association occurred with the private flagships, and positive links were found with private selective and private linking colleges. Thus, private standard colleges do not appear to be a primary source of students for private flagship and selective colleges as might have been assumed from the maximum percent overlap measure. To summarize, implications for enrollment shifts and competitive actions during a period of demographic change are very different using these two measures of competitive overlap. The differences will be equally important for describing specific competitors of individual colleges or identifying key student and college characteristics influencing competition.

Selecting Variables. The importance of selecting an appropriate association measure has just been discussed. It is equally important to consider how variables are selected. Low associations may be the by-product of not having separately analyzed market segments. If two colleges each had three distinct and equal subpopulations with each interested in distinct college groups, it is possible that complete college overlap could exist for each subpopulation. The COLES association between subpopulations of the two colleges would be 1.0. However, if the association were calculated irrespective of subpopulation, COLES for two colleges of equal size would be suppressed to 0.24. (This pattern occurs for any association measures.)

Individual colleges are typically complex entities serving groups of students with different academic, social, and economic backgrounds and different program interests. Measuring overlap in total applications to any pair of colleges should be expected to suppress overlap measures. It is reasonable to use a relatively low criterion when assessing these general competitive relationships. When focusing on a fairly specific market segment (for example, out-of-state applicants interested in a physics program), interpretation of association measures can more appropriately be made using conventional social science norms.

Inadequate variable selection may explain much of the difficulty researchers have had in identifying student characteristics that are strong predictors of students' choices of college. For example, it will be unproductive to analyze middle-inome students ($15,000–$25,000) if aid programs are such that net college cost is much different for income groups $15,000-$18,000, $18,001-$21,000, and $21,001-$25,000. If only students in the top 2 percent academically are typically eligible for or interested in certain colleges, then a categorical variable representing the top 10 percent academically may fail to reveal strong relationships. For other variables it is not as easy to know beforehand what the most useful categories for analysis are. Thus, a certain amount of exploratory research is necessary.

Failure to expose interaction effects between variables is directly related to the problem of selecting individual categorical variables. The analysis of continuous variables cannot identify nonlinear or categorical relationships for either main effects or interaction effects. The analysis of categorical variables helps only if the correct categories have been selected. "Simpson's paradox" (Simpson, 1951) refers to the situation in which a variable or set of variables (such as race or gender) may show no positive relationship with a dependent variable (College "X") until one or more additional variables (ability, personal drive) are added as controls. One specific categorical combination of those variables may be positively related to College "X" when a slightly different combination is unrelated or negatively related. "Simpson's paradox" type relationships are common when subpopulations vary widely in relative size—an apt description of institutional market segments.

Researchers must continually ask themselves whether low associations obtained in their analyses are real or a consequence of weak data and variable definition as well as inadequate association measures. Variable selection is extremely important. Increasingly, research suggests that competitive structures are more complex and strongly linked to each other and to specific student types. Given the rareness of applications to any single college and the rareness of very specific types of prospective students in the population, large or highly selective data sets may be necessary to adequately describe competitive college structures.

References

Chapman, D. "A Model of Student College Choice." *Journal of Higher Education*, 1981, *52* (5), 490-505.

Cole, L. "The Measure of Interspecific Association." *Ecology*, 1949, *30* (4), 411-424.

Fleiss, J. *Statistical Methods for Rates and Proportions*. New York: Wiley, 1981.

Glover, R. "Designing a Decision Support System for Enrollment Management." *Research in Higher Education*, 1986, *24* (1), 15-34.

Goodman, L., and Kruskal, W. *Measures of Association for Cross Classifications*. New York: Springer-Verlag, 1979.

Jackson, G. *Efficiency and Enrollment Modification in Higher Education: Project Report No. 80-A5*. Stanford, Calif.: Institute for Research on Education Finance and Governance, Stanford University, December 1980.

Litten, L. "Different Strokes in the Applicant Pool: Some Refinements in a Model of Student Choice." *Journal of Higher Education*, 1982, *53* (4), 393-402.

Muthen, B. "A General Structural Equation Model with Dichotomous, Ordered Categorical, and Continuous Laten Variable Indicators." *Psychometrika*, 1984, *49* (1), 115-132.

Reynolds, H. T. *Analysis of Nominal Data*. Beverly Hills, Calif.: Sage, 1977.

Rowse, G. "A Study of Generalized Canonical Reduction Methods for Investigating Student College Choice Correlates." Unpublished dissertation, State University of New York at Albany, December 1985.

Rowse, G., and Wing, P. "Assessing Competitive Structures in Higher Education." *Journal of Higher Education*, 1982, Nov./Dec., 656-686.

Simpson, E. H. "The Interpretation of Interaction in Contingency Tables." *Journal of the Royal Statistical Society*, 1951, *B* (8), no. 2, 238-241.

Sullivan, D., Litten, L. H., Morris, D., and Brodigan, D. "On the Structure of the Market for Higher Education in Six Cities." Paper presented to the Middle States Regional Assembly of the College Board, Philadelphia, February 1980.

Wing, P., and Rowse, G. "Coping with Competition for Students in a Period of Decline." *Planning for Higher Education*, 1986, *14* (1), 6-15.

Zemsky, R., and Oedel, P. *The Structure of College Choice*. New York: College Entrance Examination Board, 1983.

Glenwood L. Rowse is assistant bureau chief of postsecondary research at the New York State Education Department in Albany, New York.

Trade-off analysis can be a powerful tool in the assessment
of market position and exploration of repositioning options.

Positioning and Trade-Off Analysis

Eric Straumanis

Any product or service for which there is substantial demand, and which has been available in the marketplace for some time, occupies a "position" relative to other similar products or services. This is so even if the providers of the product or service are unable to describe the position precisely. As much as academic planners may resist the notion, educational institutions occupy positions in their marketplace just as commercial companies do in theirs.

Because educational institutions do not provide products per se, the relevant non-educational marketing analogue for them is the nonprofit service organization, a library or museum, for instance. If an institution is diverse, then some of its constituent programs might occupy distinct positions in their respective markets. For example, a master of business administration (MBA) program may occupy a market position distinctly different from that of its parent institution.

Position means location with respect to characteristics or attributes important to users and producers of the service. The attributes can be objective (cost, size, and advertising expenditures, for example), or subjective (perceived cost, prestige, reputation, quality, and the like). The market position of a service is usually multidimensional and competitive: More than one attribute determines demand, and there are multiple providers in

R. S. Lay and J. J. Endo (eds.). *Designing and Using Market Research.*
New Directions for Institutional Research, no. 54. San Francisco: Jossey-Bass, Summer 1987.

the marketplace. A useful technique for graphing market position is to choose the three most important attributes to represent the axes of a graph, and then assign each competitor a point in the graph according to how its service "scores" on the chosen attributes. Figure 1 displays the positions occupied by MBA programs in a market space defined by the dimensions of cost, convenience, and prestige.

There is a vast literature on techniques for describing and representing market structure. Shocker (1986) provides a taxonomy of techniques with a recent bibliography. A graph using three attributes such as that in Figure 1 can be the result of a multistage survey data collection and analytic reduction process, or it can be constructed from relatively easily gathered expert opinion data. Time and resource constraints and amount of prior knowledge about one's relative market position will determine how much effort is to be devoted to this task. The resulting market map or "space" should be represented by no more than three attributes, otherwise it is not likely to be understood by decision makers.

Successful strategic planning requires more than just locating your institution in competitive market space—it also requires determining the direction to attempt to move the institution. A thorough discussion of available techniques can be found in Urban and Hauser (1980). Conjoint or trade-off analysis (TOA), the research technique described in this chapter, can be very helpful in making this determination. TOA is usually applied *after* a competitive environment has been initially analyzed and described; as a repositioning tool, TOA belongs to the later stages of the process of positioning research and planning.

Figure 1. MBA Program Positions in Attribute Space

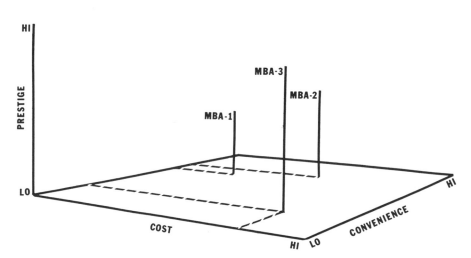

Repositioning

There are two important reasons for knowing the position one's institution or program occupies in the academic marketplace. First, it can help explain past enrollment management successes and failures, and second, it should be the basis for any repositioning strategy one might adopt. Here we will be concerned only with the second of these issues.

To reposition a program is to change the perception of it by key publics on some or all of the attributes used to locate its current position in the market. What are typical reasons for repositioning? A declining market, together with an unwillingness to reduce enrollments, is indicative of a need to reposition in order to maintain market share. Or if the demographic and competitive forces are favorable, repositioning might aim at increasing market share, or perhaps at increasing it only in higher-quality client segments. In the commercial domain, client or customer quality is measured by how likely the customers are to purchase future service expansions, and by their responsiveness if prices are increased. In higher education, client quality is more complex because the consumer is also a major contributor to the value of the services provided. In assessing the quality of different prospective student pools, we must not only consider how likely students are to enroll but also their academic abilities, skills, and attainments. Nevertheless, the institution's *expected market share* will probably be one of the key criteria in choosing from among several repositioning strategies.

To continue with the example depicting the various positions occupied by MBA programs in a market space defined by the attributes of cost, convenience, and prestige, it is clear that the "line of ideal preference" for prospective MBA students is in the direction of increasing convenience and prestige and decreasing cost. The MBA program capable of delivering the most prestige and convenience at the lowest cost would eventually capture the largest market share. But what would be ideal for prospective students is usually not economically feasible for the institution. Very large resources are needed to finance a repositioning move along the ideal line. The investment required to improve prestige might not be repaid by resulting gains in market share in the valued student segments. A realistic repositioning option for improving the market position of the MBA program might well be a modest or incremental move, not necessarily along the ideal preference line. To pick the option with the best payoff requires finding out which of the less than ideal, but feasible, moves would cause the largest increase in student preference. We have to raise and answer questions such as, "How large an increase in cost will prospective students find acceptable in order to gain how large an improvement in prestige (or convenience)?" In answering questions such as these TOA techniques can make their special contribution to positioning research.

In one sense the idea of repositioning is not new to higher education. Well before the recent popularity of marketing, institutions changed costs, program content, and other key factors in response to what they sensed as, but did not explicitly describe as, market forces. Though the concept is not new, until recently it has been applied in higher education without benefit of repositioning techniques used in the business sector. Higher education today is faced with managing a portfolio of programs, some of which may be losing enrollments. A repositioning decision grounded only in enlightened intuition and practical experience is too risky. It is far wiser, for example, to raise tuition and shift program emphasis only after having systematically explored or simulated the marketplace effects of alternative moves. The TOA technique can provide a degree of power and precision too often untapped in educational program decision making.

Trade-Off Analysis as a Repositioning Tool

One way to begin an explanation of TOA is to contrast *conjoint* with *disjoint*, a term which describes the usual way of soliciting evaluative responses from respondents. Many academic institutions have conducted surveys asking for ratings of the importance and attractiveness of program characteristics. Attributes such as quality of faculty, intellectual atmosphere, and student social life have been typical items evaluated. Respondents have been asked to rate these in the abstract and to consider one attribute at a time, or disjointly. The problem with this approach is that it lacks specificity and realism. From such ratings we are unable to determine how much of a particular attribute (say, convenience) a person would be willing to give up or trade off in favor of how large an improvement in another attribute (say, cost). But real-life choices are made precisely in such specific contexts. As an illustration of how TOA preserves specificity and realism we will describe the main elements of the Suffolk University MBA Study.

Suffolk University Study of MBA Students

Rationale and Design of the Study. Our main objective was to develop a research basis for formulating and evaluating various repositioning options for the MBA program. There are at least a dozen MBA programs offered in the greater Boston area. Some draw students on a regional or national basis, overlapping less with institutions that draw mainly from metropolitan Boston. We knew from experience and other research that Suffolk University's primary competition for Boston area MBAs consists of four institutions.

We felt that TOA was the tool of choice for achieving our research objective. Our reasons for that choice will illustrate some of the strengths and limitations of TOA. As Riedesel (1985) has noted, the theory underlying TOA assumes that people behave rationally, that they will choose the product or service that best meets their needs and values. TOA also assumes that people will make choices in the light of fairly complete information. The degree to which these assumptions hold will vary, depending on the service and the market. In a predominantly urban, employed, older or returning student market where people tend to seek a practical degree such as the MBA, these assumptions will be met. That is, the student's choice of MBA program is very likely a rational self-interested decision made in the light of reasonably complete information. In some traditional private four-year liberal arts college markets these assumptions might not be met to the same degree. For example, if a survey of accepted applicants reveals that a large proportion of enrolling students greatly overrated key attributes of the institution, there is reason to believe their choice was not fully rational and informed. Whether or not the rationality assumptions of TOA are met within acceptable bounds in any given student market is, in the final analysis, a judgment call.

At Suffolk University, we decided to use a microcomputer-based approach for both data gathering and analysis. The mode of implementation does not fundamentally affect the research rationale described here. For advantages and limitations of this approach, see the Methodological Appendix at the end of the chapter, where the practical aspects of conducting surveys by microcomputer are discussed.

The TOA rating tasks were performed by a sample of enrolled MBA students, 119 (21 percent) of whom returned usable responses. No response bias was found using variables in the student data file, but some of the nonresponse seems to have been caused by the requirement to use a computer, possibly grounds for thinking there might be response bias on some of the items in the study. Therefore, the results should be used with caution, but they provide a useful illustration of the TOA technique.

Attributes, Profile Ratings, and Utility Scores. As explained earlier, before a TOA can be set up, it is necessary to identify the dimensions that define the market space for one's institution and its principal competitors (the "competition set"). If the institution has not recently conducted an accepted applicant survey containing evaluative items on the enrollment decision, then there might not be an adequate basis for defining the market space for the competition set. Even when recent survey data are available, they might not have received the analysis necessary for identifying the key dimensions for market space definition. (The usual technique is to factor analyze the institutional attribute ratings. This makes it possible to collapse or reduce a large number of attributes to a manageable number of key dimensions that can be used to define the market space.) Survey research that results in the description of the competition set can be expensive and time consuming, but it is highly advisable for undergraduate institutions who have never gone through the process. The short-cut alternative is to rely on qualitative techniques such as the gathering of expert opinions (admissions staff and faculty), supplemented with so-called focus groups of appropriately selected students (enrolling and non-enrolling accepted applicants, for example). The qualitative approach is justifiable for positioning research on graduate or professional programs if reliable and credible results about the market structure of the competition set are obtained.

Because of time and resource constraints, Suffolk University decided to use the results of some earlier focus group research on MBAs, together with the expert opinions of graduate admissions recruiters. Five attributes, each allowing from five to nine different ranked responses, emerged as the likely basis for the enrollment decisions prospective MBA students made. These five attributes also serve as the dimensions for defining Suffolk's MBA market space.

Notice that the often used "quality of . . ." attributes such as quality of program and quality of faculty do not appear in Table 1. This is intended to avoid violating the independence and noninteraction assumptions of conjoint analysis. Quality of program would surely overlap quality of students or quality of faculty. My colleagues and I let "quality" reside in attributes formulated as much as possible in terms of benefits; for example, value of the degree and faculty attention. We tried to guard against the interaction of cost with notions of quality by explicitly instructing respondents to evaluate cost according to their financial needs or preferences only—to avoid assuming that lower cost is indicative of lower quality.

The five attributes with specified levels were the building blocks from which different hypothetical MBA program profiles were constructed by the computer program. Profiles were presented in pairs, with respondents having to rate on a nine-point scale their degree of preference of one hypothetical MBA program over the other. Again, what makes this rating task conjoint rather than disjoint is that all of the key elements involved in the student's choice of MBA program are being presented simultaneously. Table 2 shows an example of a profile pair and the rating scale presented on the computer screen. (After making a preference decision, the respondent presses the appropriate scale number on the keyboard.)

The computer program builds profile pairs for screen presentation as the "interview" progresses. The number of pairs a respondent is given for evaluation and the particular mix of attribute rankings (or levels) that appear depends on answers that person gave to prior calibrating questions and profile rating questions. Between twenty-four and thirty profiles have to be rated by a respondent in order to complete the TOA task. Not all screens contain profiles as "realistic" as the two in Table 2 because the TOA program must systematically cover the range of possible alternatives. However, to make the rating task practically manageable, it is necessary to reduce the number of combinations presented to respondents. This is called "fractional factorial design" and is described in Green, Carroll, and Carmone (1978).

Table 1. Attributes, Levels, and Utility Scores

		Utility
Tuition:	$3,000-$5,000/year	60
	$5,001-$7,000/year	25
	$7,001-$9,000/year	13
	$9,001-$11,000/year	6
	$11,001 or more/year	2
Value	Very high probability of high income	53
of Degree:	High probability of high income	37
	Fair probability of high income	12
	Uncertain probability of high income	3
	Low probability of high income	1
Convenience:	10 minutes or less	37
	10-20 minutes to campus	27
	20-30 minutes to campus	15
	30-45 minutes to campus	7
	45-60 minutes to campus	4
	more than 60 minutes	0
Curriculum	Theoretical—HIGH / Practical—HIGH	40
Emphasis:	Theoretical—HIGH / Practical—MED	13
	Theoretical—HIGH / Practical—LOW	1
	Theoretical—MED / Practical—HIGH	42
	Theoretical—MED / Practical—MED	14
	Theoretical—MED / Practical—LOW	1
	Theoretical—LOW / Practical—HIGH	12
	Theoretical—LOW / Practical—MED	3
Faculty	Outstanding	36
Attention:	Very strong	23
	Strong	12
	Fair	1
	Barely adequate	1
	Almost none	0

When the rating task is complete, the computer program calculates utility scores for each respondent for each attribute level—see Table 1. For technical explanations of the algorithms used, see *ACA System . . .* (1986) and Green (1984). The meaning of utilities or utility scores can be made intuitive by stating what utilities are *not*. A utility score should not be thought of as a rating of usefulness that a respondent assigns to a particular attribute during the TOA task. Recall that during the TOA task respondents assign preference ratings to program profiles. The utility score represents the mathematically calculated value or preference weight that an attribute or feature has for a respondent, given the set of profile preference ratings that were generated from all that subject's responses during the TOA task.

Utility scores are calculated so as to best explain or recover the

Table 2. Sample Profile with Rating Scale

Program A

Strongly Prefer Top	Tuition:	$5,001–$7,000 per year
	Value of Degree:	Fair probability of high income
1	Convenience:	20–30 minutes to campus
2	Curriculum Emphasis:	Theoretical—MEDIUM
3		Practical—HIGH
4	Faculty Attention:	Fair

5 — OR —

Program B

6	Tuition:	$9,001–$11,000 per year
7	Value of Degree:	High probability of high income
8	Convenience:	30–45 minutes to campus
9	Curriculum Emphasis:	Theoretical—HIGH
Strongly Prefer Bottom		Practical—MEDIUM
	Faculty Attention:	Strong

program profile rankings that result from the rating task. A very important property of these utility scores is that they are additive. The total utility of (or aggregated preference for) an actual or hypothetical MBA program can be determined by adding up the individual utility scores, feature by feature.

For example, Program A in Table 2 would receive a total utility score of 95 and Program B a score of 75, calculated from the average utilities listed in Table 1. Such a result might not have been predicted without using this technique. The fact that scores are also calculated for each respondent means that, given a segmentable group of respondents, average utility scores for various programs can be calculated for segments on the basis of sex, test scores, competitor action on application, full-time or part-time status, employment, tuition support by employer, or whatever available variable is thought to have marketing significance.

Market Simulation and Repositioning Options

After utility scores have been calculated, it is relatively easy to simulate different market environments for an institution and its competition. It is best to start with a simplified model: the institution to be repositioned plus its top two competitors.

Each competitor to be entered into the simulation must first be described or profiled in terms of the attributes listed in Table 1. Ideally, such profiles should be obtained by surveying representative samples of the populations of interest—prospective MBA students or accepted MBA applicants who decided to enroll at competitor schools. Because of resource limitations, we took the qualitative approach here as well—by soliciting expert judgments from faculty and graduate admissions personnel. This short-cut is less problematic than the one described earlier. Experts are more likely to correctly rate competitors on specified attributes than they are to correctly identify the attributes that define the market space for a competition set.

When the initial attribute descriptions for each institution have been entered, the market simulator (a module in the Sawtooth ACA computer program—see Methodological Appendix) calculates the shares of preference each institution could expect in the respondent group. To perform the calculation, the program relies on the utility scores computed earlier. An institution's preference share can be considered as its predicted market share, the percentage of the specified student market that would enroll if choice behavior were in perfect accord with stated preference. Because the initial program descriptions are assumed to represent the current competitor relationships in the market, the initial preference share distribution is called the "base case," against which various "what if" or simulated repositioning options can be compared. These elements are graphically displayed in Figure 2.

Figure 2. Repositioning Options and Preference Shares

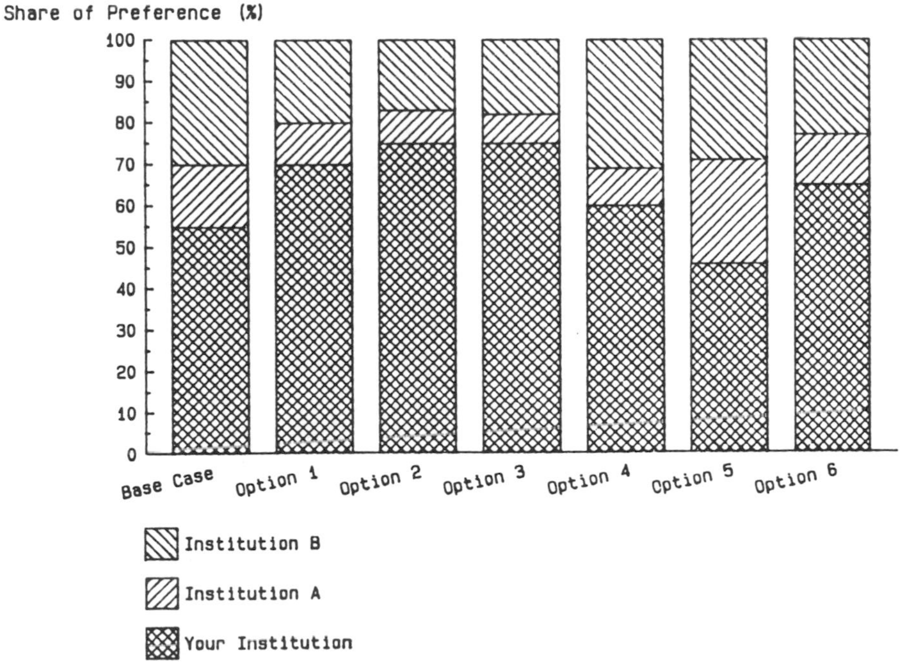

Share of Preference (%)

Base Case Option 1 Option 2 Option 3 Option 4 Option 5 Option 6

Institution B
Institution A
Your Institution

The base case bar indicates that Your Institution currently enjoys a 55 percent share of preference. The six stacked bars to the right of base case show which preference share shifts among the three modeled competitors can be expected if changes in program attributes (not specified in Figure 2) were to be made. Notice that for options 1, 2, 3, 4, and 6 the market share for Your Institution increases over the base case; for option 5 it drops below the base case level of 55 percent. It is clear that option 5 is not desirable, but a great deal of "what if" sensitivity testing is likely to be required before the analyst settles on a candidate set of viable options worth consideration by policy makers. Sensitivity testing refers to the process of systematically varying the level of an attribute in order to determine the effect of the changes on the preference shares emerging from the model. For instance, one might step through all the levels of curriculum emphasis (except the one already specified in the base case) to discover how the preference share for Your Institution shifts in response to the different simulated changes.

If certain simulated changes improve your share of preference and are within the capabilities of Your Institution to implement, they can be considered as realistic repositioning options. For example, in Figure 2, option 2 is the result of changing curriculum emphasis from "Theoretical—LOW; Practical—HIGH" to "Theoretical—MEDIUM; Practical—HIGH." A 20 percentage-point increase in preference share can be expected as a result of this move. However, it might be very difficult to achieve such an ideal curriculum mix.

Finally, market simulation need not be restricted to "what ifs" based on changes in attributes of Your Institution. Changes competitors might make in response to market forces can also be simulated. For example, the preference share distribution in option 3 is the result of a tuition increase by Institution B and a curriculum emphasis change in Your Institution. Because the number of different combinations that can be simulated on the computer is virtually limitless, the analyst and the decision maker could gain a great deal by spending some time together at the computer keyboard.

Conclusion

The development of TOA has occurred primarily in the design of new commercial products and services—in helping management select the characteristics that best link the service to consumer preference. Repositioning an academic institution or one of its constituent programs can be seen as structurally similar to introducing a new or modified service. The leadership of the institution should be aware of the trade-offs when contemplating a shift in curriculum emphasis, tuition, or investment in teaching resources. The application of TOA techniques can reveal the combination of major factors that would maximize preference in selected student markets. Of course, institutions of higher education, much more so than commercial organizations, must also deal with a difficult normative question: Is it *educationally* desirable to reposition so as to maximize prospective student preference? Research cannot provide an answer to that question.

Methodological Appendix

Comparison of Personal Interview with Microcomputer Approaches. Until very recently, the standard way to conduct TOA studies was to use cue cards. Each card has a different product or service profile printed on it. A trained interviewer is required to present card pairs, record responses, and shuffle the deck at the appropriate stages. When the complexity of profiles is moderate or great, raters want to proceed at different speeds. Hence, even small groups present problems for the interviewer. Most important, appointments have to be made and kept, and appropriate interviewing facilities are required. On the plus side, no special equipment is needed and, given that TOA data gathering is more complicated than a mail survey, the interviewer's presence can prevent respondent frustration and the collection of bad data.

Currently there are several microcomputer software packages available for TOA studies. (See the software review that follows.) There are a number of major advantages in using this automated approach. First, the sequencing and specific content of profile pairs can be optimized because the computer, unlike the human interviewer, can instantly utilize information from preceding responses. Second, subjects can perform the task at their own pace and at a time of their choosing because the interview portion of the software can usually be made to fit on a single floppy disk. Third, background and non-TOA evaluative data can be collected during the same interview as TOA data. Fourth, no additional data entry step is required—all data are available for analysis as soon as enough respondents have completed the task.

There are, however, some disadvantages and limitations to using microcomputers for TOA studies. First and most obviously, subjects without convenient access to a compatible micro are likely to be excluded. But this state of affairs is in rapid change for the better. A few universities have already equipped their dormitories for micros. Most universities have micro labs where a group session with respondents who are not computer literate could be set up. This case is no worse than having to arrange a group interview using the traditional approach. Of course the computer-phobic may still be unreachable.

Second, the level of computer competence required of the researcher running the study has to be high. Even when the software is user-friendly, as was the case in our study, all sorts of problems in running the programs on mail-out or field floppies are bound to occur. These are often caused by a respondent's failure to understand the operating system of the machine being used. The study directors must be capable of solving such problems over the phone.

Software Review. Conjoint analysis has been in use long enough for the development of a sizable body of software. This brief review makes no claim to being complete. The available software can be roughly divided into two categories: (1) university-based and aimed primarily at academic researchers and (2) intended for the commercial market researcher. As a general rule, using the first category of software requires deeper methodological understanding than using the second category, which tends to be more user-friendly but often is incomplete in its description of methodology. As with any advanced technique, the TOA user should have as complete an understanding as possible. However, careful following of the documentation of the second category of software will at least carry the neophyte from start to finish. With a product from the first category, progress for the inexperienced will be slower. Products differ in terms of the features they provide; no attempt is made to document such differences here.

In the first category the most important product has been LINMAP, which has gone through multiple versions (Srinivasan and Shocker, 1982). Others in this category are MKTSHR (Wiley and Low, 1979), MULTI-CON (Gates, 1982), CONJOINT (Smith, 1985), and CHOISIM (Lambert, Mathur, and Reddy, 1985).

In the second category there are products differing in scope. CON-JOINT DESIGNER (1985), recently reviewed in Carmone (1986), appears to have high ease of use without requiring detailed understanding of experimental design. ACA (1986) produced by Sawtooth Software works in conjunction with their CI2 (computer interviewing) module. (For a recent review, see Smith, 1986.) The advantage of a TOA or conjoint package that can be linked with an interview module is that segmentation and conjoint data can be obtained in the same session.

The Suffolk MBA Study used the Sawtooth products. The associated CI2 module had to be customized to contain survey questions in the sequence and with the branching desired. We found this a straightforward, though time-consuming task. The ACA module had to be configured with the attribute and level information for doing this, but anyone skilled with a text editor can by-pass these and create the required frames directly. The logic of presentation in the ACA module is not alterable; however, it is flexibly designed to adapt to the subject's responses. The market simulation feature of the ACA is menu-driven, is quite user-friendly, and contains various options for altering the course of the simulations. After having worked through one study, our overall judgment is that the package is very competently executed, but not polished. Given that it is aimed at the commercial user, the documentation has a somewhat home-made quality, but it is reasonably detailed and informative. Most of the statistical assumptions of the ACA module are explained or at least mentioned. But since conjoint analysis involves more than basic statistics, users should have a deeper understanding of the issues that can be gleaned from the manual provided with the software.

Models of Preference Formation, Methods of Parameter Estimation, Robustness, and Other Design Characteristics. Because conjoint analysis has been widely used in commercial market research during the past fifteen years, several approaches differing in formal and structural properties have emerged. There are five criteria on which conjoint procedures can differ: selection of a model of preference, data collection, profile set construction and presentation, measurement scale, and estimation method. A good overview of these can be found in Green and Srinivasan (1978). Discussions of validity and robustness also abound in the literature. There is considerable agreement among authors that TOA is robust under a variety of threats. For details consult Green and Srinivasan (1978), Segal (1982), Carmone, Green, and Jain (1978), and Leigh, MacKay, and Summers (1984).

References

ACA System for Conjoint Analysis: Documentation. Ketchum, Idaho: Sawtooth Software, 1986.

Carmone, F. J. "Review of Conjoint Designer." *Journal of Marketing Research,* 1986, *23* (8), 311–312.

Carmone, F. J., Green, P. E., and Jain, A. K. "Robustness of Conjoint Analysis: Some Monte Carlo Results." *Journal of Marketing Research,* 1978, *15* (5), 300.

Conjoint Designer. New York: Bretton-Clark, 1985.

Gates, R. "MULTICON: A Program for Doing Conjoint Analysis Via User-Selected Algorithm." *Journal of Marketing Research,* 1982, *19* (11), 604–605.

Green, P. E. "Hybrid Models for Conjoint Analysis: An Expository Review." *Journal of Marketing Research,* 1984, *21* (5), 155–169.

Green, P. E., Carroll, J. D., and Carmone, F. J. "Some New Types of Fractional Factorial Designs for Marketing Experiments." In J. N. Sheth (ed.), *Research in Marketing.* Greenwich, Conn.: JAI Press, 1978.

Green, P. E., and Srinivasan, V. "Conjoint Analysis in Consumer Research: Issues and Outlook." *Journal of Consumer Research,* 1978, *3* (9), 103–123.

Lambert, D. A., Mathur, K., and Reddy, N. H. "CHOISIM: A First-Choice Simulator for Conjoint Scaled Data." *Journal of Marketing Research,* 1985, *22* (5), 219–221.

Leigh, T. W., MacKay, D. B., and Summers, J. O. "Reliability and Validity of Conjoint Analysis and Self-Explicated Weights: A Comparison." *Journal of Marketing Research,* 1984, *21* (11), 456.

Riedesel, P. L. "Conjoint Analysis Is Worthwhile Tool, But Be Sure Data Are Valid." *Marketing News,* September 13, 1985, p. 36.

Segal, M. N. "Reliability of Conjoint Analysis: Contrasting Data Collection Procedures." *Journal of Marketing Research,* 1982, *19* (19), 139–143.

Shocker, A. D. "Competitive Relationships Must Be Viewed from Customer Perspectives." *Marketing Educator,* 1986, *5* (3), 4–5.

Smith, S. M. "CONJOINT: Conjoint Statistical Analysis." *Journal of Marketing Research,* 1985, *22* (5), 221–222.

74

Smith, S. M. "Review of CI2 System." *Journal of Marketing Research*, 1986, *23* (2), 84–85.

Srinivasan, V., and Shocker, A. D. "LINMAP (Version IV): A FORTRAN IV Computer Program for Analyzing Ordinal Preference Judgments for Conjoint and Trade-Off Analyses." *Journal of Marketing Research*, 1982, *11*, 601–602.

Urban, G. L., and Hauser, J. R. *Design and Marketing of New Products.* Englewood Cliffs, N.J.: Prentice-Hall, 1980.

Wiley, J. B., and Low, J. T. "MKTSHR: Market Share Analysis—A Program for Estimating Market Shares from Conjoint Analysis Data." *Journal of Marketing Research*, 1979, *16* (11), 568.

Eric Straumanis is director of enrollment research at Suffolk University in Boston.

Understanding prospective students' perceptions of college prices and educational quality can ease some of the strain associated with setting institutional price. This chapter describes how to gather and interpret perceptual data.

Balancing Price and Value

David L. Brodigan

A very difficult and worrisome task for trustees and administrators at independent colleges and universities—the setting of the comprehensive fee—has grown more complex in recent years. The complexity of the task has increased because a growing assortment of factors, often pushing in opposite directions, must be recognized and understood. Decreasing numbers of high school graduates, declining federal support for financial aid programs, changing market demand, institutional aspirations, and increasing costs of educational resources are some of the factors that must be considered. Prominent among the educational resources that are increasing in cost is faculty, and falling behind in the competition for a first-rate faculty must be avoided if educational quality is to be maintained. At the same time, price increases that move beyond the ability or willingness of families to pay are hazardous to institutional well-being. In this climate, significant knowledge of the views of prospective students regarding college price, quality, and value would be most useful, but unfortunately, that information is usually not available.

In order to avoid setting its comprehensive fee in the absence of this kind of information, Carleton College began several years ago to develop a research technique that would permit measurement of prospective students' perceptions of college price and educational quality. Somewhat unexpectedly, Carleton College found attitudes concerning educational value to be reflected in the relation between those dimensions. The purpose of this

R. S. Lay and J. J. Endo (eds.). *Designing and Using Market Research.*
New Directions for Institutional Research, no. 54. San Francisco: Jossey-Bass, Summer 1987.

chapter is to describe that technique and to present examples of results that may be of general interest to the broad educational community.

Terminology: Price, Quality, and Value

In order to avoid unnecessary complexity during the initial stages of this research effort, let us say that college price is synonymous with comprehensive fee. Only the institutionally stated total of tuition, fees, and room and board charges have been considered. Certainly, price could be defined in more complex ways. For example, the availability of college grants (either financial aid or merit awards) might be included in the equation. Litten (1984) offers a variety of perspectives, varying in complexity, on higher education price and pricing issues.

Realizing that among prospective students opinions and judgments about educational quality are commonplace, but that notions about the basic elements and determinants of educational quality are not uniform, a strict definition for that entity was not adopted. We at Carleton College were, of course, interested in knowing more about the nature of educational quality as the students saw it, but our strategy was to set that question aside until significant progress was made in the measurement of the perception of educational quality.

Estimates of value are based on the relative levels of perceived quality and perceived price. In one instance, an institution perceived to have a relatively low price and relatively high quality may be thought of as an excellent educational value, while in another case, having perceived quality that is commensurate with perceived price may be a good value. When perceived quality falls below perceived price and the difference is large, relatively little educational value is thought to be present.

Methodology

The research technique I employed for the Carleton College study is called magnitude estimation, and it was originally developed by psychologists for the purpose of studying human perceptual dimensions for environmental stimuli (for example, the brightness of light and the intensity of sound). The technique can be used to scale human perceptual responses to any metric stimulus (for example, dolllars), and it can be applied to the quantitative measurement of nonmetric social stimuli as well (see Lodge, 1981, for an introduction to magnitude scaling). As I adapted it, the basic methodology required the presentation of a list of college names along with instructions that numeric estimates of the relative price (or quality) be assigned to each institution. Additional details concerning these magnitude estimation procedures will be described in the presentation and interpretation of samples of my research findings, but more general background is needed first.

The figures that appear in this chapter show the relative positions of institutions along two dimensions. The actual prices of the institutions are represented on the x-axis, while institutional positions on the perceptual dimension appear along the y-axis. The scales on the axes are logarithmic, and a straight line is drawn to show the least squares best fit. The relationship can be represented as log linear because of the empirical observation in the study of human perception that the relation between stimulus intensity and the subjective sensation of stimulus intensity is described by the power law, $R = S^n$. If we say that R is the subjective response to the stimulus, k is a constant depending on the unit of measurement, and S is the magnitude of the stimulus, in logarithmic terms, the equation is written $\log(R) = \log(k) + n\log(S)$. In this case, the log of the response is related linearly to n times the log of the stimulus plus a constant, log k. The slope, n, describes the relation between the stimulus dimension and the perceptual response. When n is less than one, the perceptual dimension contracts near the high end of the stimulus dimension (the power function plotted in ordinary linear terms is concave downward), and when n is greater than one, the psychological response grows at a rate that is greater than the actual rate of growth in stimulus size (the power function's exponent is greater than one, and its plot in linear coordinates is concave upward).

The slope of the line, representing the linear relation between college price and the perceptual dimension of price or quality, is used in three ways. First, it is a convenient way of summarizing the observed relations between the perceptual dimensions and the college price dimension. Second, it provides a means of comparing the perceptual dimensions of price and quality with each other, and finally, the slope can be used to characterize and compare the responses of different groups of prospective students or market segments.

Past Experience and Basic Findings

Among the fundamental principles we have come to know through past applications of this methodology are the following: First, when students are familiar with a large percentage of the institutions on the list, the rate of change on the perceptual dimension is constant across the full range of prices. In other words, a difference of $200 between two relatively inexpensive schools is the same perceptually as a $200 difference between two schools at the high end of the continuum, when students are familiar with the schools presented. When familiarity is lacking, the relation can take other forms.

A second lesson comes from the observation that the perceptual results for some schools are consistently out of line relative to the perceptual responses to other institutions and relative to their own positions on the actual price dimension. This kind of observation has led to the conclusion that special circumstances can have a profound influence on the perceived price of some institutions. For example, a heavily endowed institution such as Rice University, which has held its price down over a long period while maintaining high quality in its programs and facilities, may give the impression of high price and high quality relative to its position on the dimension of actual price.

An earlier report (Brodigan and Sullivan, 1985) described the use of magnitude estimation procedures to answer the following questions for Carleton: How does the perception of Carleton's price compare with the perceived price of other private institutions? Does the perception of Carleton's price vary for different geographical segments of the market? Do those who choose to attend Carleton differ, in the way they perceive price and quality, from those whose interest goes no further than an inquiry about admission? How does perceived price relate to perceived quality for different segments of the market? In general, that research permitted Carleton to understand its market niche more clearly than ever before. At the national level that niche is one of comparatively high perceived quality and relatively low perceived price. Closer to home, the perception of Carleton's quality is high for students who enroll, but the price is perceived to be comparatively high also.

Looking Beyond the Current Market Niche

These findings provide examples of the kind of knowledge that administrators and trustees find helpful when faced with the task of setting the comprehensive fee. However, the problem for the researcher providing the information is to consider whether the question has been examined closely enough; can the power of the microscope be turned up and finer details be revealed? With respect to the prospective students who make inquiries about admission but fail to submit applications, one might ask whether the perceptions of some students would be more relevant to our concerns than those of others. One might, for example, want to regard those students who have submitted Scholastic Aptitude Test (SAT) scores to be a substantially more interested group of prospective students who, if conditions were right, would be more likely to become applicants. In other words, if we are trying to increase the number of applications submitted, we might wish to assign greater weight to score submitter's perceptions of our relative price and educational quality than we do to the views of other prospective students.

As another means of deepening our insight into the market, we might consider making finer geographical breakdowns in our analyses of perceptions. The largest single geographical market for Carleton is Minnesota, and within that area it may be worthwhile to compare prospective students on the basis of two categories of residential origin: (1) the metropolitan area of Minneapolis and St. Paul and (2) the rest of the state, which is made up of smaller communities and rural areas.

With these concerns (among others) in mind, I conducted a survey of "nonapplicants"—prospective applicants who made inquiries about admission to Carleton but who did not apply. The sample consisted of all nonapplicants who had submitted scores to Carleton and an additional number, selected randomly, who had not submitted scores. While the general purpose of the survey was to learn about the reasons for not submitting applications for admission to Carleton, magnitude estimation items were included so that detailed analyses of price and quality issues could be made.

The magnitude estimation, section 4, of the questionnaire, entitled "College Price Impressions" (Brodigan, 1986) contained the following instructions:

> Write a number (not dollar amount) after each of the following schools to indicate your impression of relative costs, including tuition and room and board but excluding travel expenses. To form a reference point, a response (100) for Carleton has been entered. The remaining schools are to be assigned numbers by you. If, for example, your perception is that the next school on the list is one and one half times as expensive, enter 150; on the other hand, if you see it as about half as expensive, assign it the number 50. Proceed through the list, comparing each school with Carleton, but do not spend more than a brief moment thinking about any school; rather write down the first response that occurs to you, even if you are not well acquainted with the school. If you do not recognize the name, leave that space blank and go on to the next school.

Similar instructions were used to ask for magnitude estimates for quality in section 6, entitled "Impressions of Educational Quality" (Brodigan, 1986). In part, those instructions were worded as follows:

> To form a reference point, assign a number indicating your impression of Carleton's educational quality relative to its cost. That number should be 100, if you think that the educational quality of Carleton is commensurate with its cost; otherwise adjust the number upward or downward from 100.

This instruction represents an important departure from my past survey instructions for magnitude estimation. Its purpose is to obtain a better understanding of the way the perceptual dimensions of price and quality relate to each other for Carleton, specifically. In the past, the list of institutions began with the assigned value of 100 for Carleton, and that anchor precluded any possibility of determining whether Carleton's quality was viewed as high or low in relation to its cost.

New Findings and New Market Insights

Carleton's Eastern Market. This market was composed of non-applicants residing in eleven eastern states and the District of Columbia, some of whom did and some of whom did not submit SAT scores. Very little difference was found between the two subgroups' perceptions of price as compared with the actual price of Carleton and seventeen peer institutions.

The major differences between those who submitted scores and those who did not appear on the perceptual dimension of educational quality, and they can be seen by comparing figures 1 and 2. Observe that, among those who submitted scores (Figure 1), Carleton's educational quality is seen to be as good as or better than that of nearly any other school. Furthermore, for that group Carleton's perceived quality is greater than 2.0, the score that would be obtained if its quality were merely commensurate with its price. This is a very important finding because it provides reassurance about the balance between Carleton's price and its level of perceived quality. It also provides the impetus for a closer examination of the reasons these prospective students did not apply to Carleton and for thinking about ways applications might be elicited.

To take this analysis of perceptions one step further, the quality and price estimates are plotted together in figures 3 and 4. The purpose of this exercise is to assess educational value as it is reflected in the differences between these estimates. The broken line in these figures is the least squares best fit that would occur if price and quality were rated for every school. The deviation of the actual least-squares-best-fit line (the unbroken line) from the broken line indicates the extent to which educational quality is not viewed as commensurate with price.

The difference between the two groups is very large; those who submit scores do not see the quality of the more expensive schools as commensurate with their prices; for these students, educational value is to be found in schools that cost less. To be sure, for both groups there are schools that are viewed as having lower educational quality than one would expect given the high perceived price of the institutions, and there are other institutions that are perceived to offer more educational quality than might be expected. With respect to the score-submitting group, Carleton is positioned in the portion of the graph indicating comparatively good perceived educational value. However, the fact that several

**Figure 1. Quality Perception of Eastern Nonapplicants:
Scores Submitted**

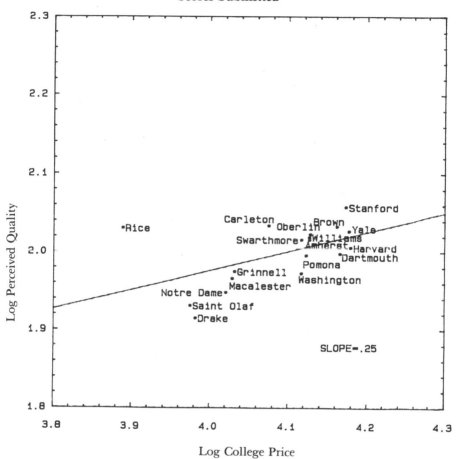

other schools have the same appearance for these students must not be overlooked. Any reassurance about price that we might take from Carleton's especially favorable position with this group has to be tempered with the knowledge that other schools occupy similar positions and, undoubtedly, share the benefits of this market niche.

One of the larger questions about the balance between price and quality that we hope to answer with data of this kind is as follows: Have recent college price increases, at rates substantially greater than the rate of inflation, changed the way prospective students perceive price? Or have the increases changed the way students think about the amount of educational quality they will receive for their money? Because in 1983 Carleton conducted a survey of prospective students who made inquiries but did

Figure 2. Quality Perception of Eastern Nonapplicants:
No Scores Submitted

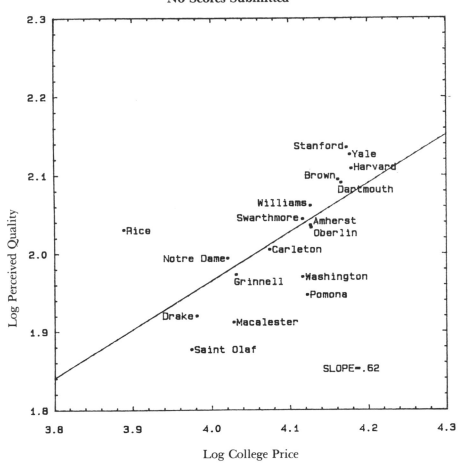

not submit applications, and because measurements of perceived price and quality were obtained on that occasion, the following observations can be offered.

Overall, comparisons of the results of the two surveys indicate that the relative positions of the schools have not changed greatly along the perceptual dimension for college price. The slope of the plot for the 1986 nonapplicants of the eastern region differs very little from that observed in 1983, and the general relations between the institutions on the list have remained constant.

However, a major and potentially very important change along the perceptual dimension of quality has occurred. In 1983 the slope of the least-squares-best-fit line for perception of quality was 0.99 for eastern

Figure 3. Price and Quality Perception of Eastern Nonapplicants:
Scores Submitted

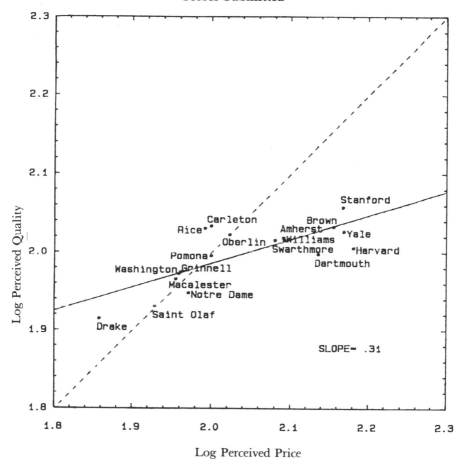

nonapplicants, and there was every indication that quality was viewed as commensurate with price. Judging from the results presented in figures 1 through 4, that is not the dominant view today. This difference may mean that the dramatic price increases of recent years have changed the way some students think about the value of the higher-priced schools. This finding should be regarded as potentially very important and should not be ignored by administrators and trustees. Recent price increases, and the unfavorable publicity that has accompanied them, may be having serious market consequences.

For Carleton's future well-being, the shift between 1983 and 1986, if it represents growth in the number of people who feel that high-quality education can be obtained at a comparatively low price, may actually

84

Figure 4. Price and Quality Perception of Eastern Nonapplicants:
No Scores Submitted

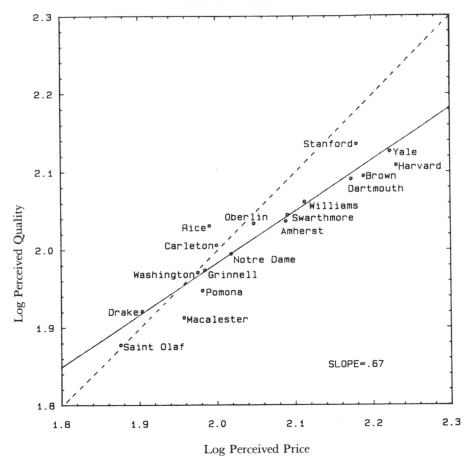

mean increasing demand and improving opportunities for admissions success. For other educational institutions, and for those on the high end of the real price continuum in particular, the consequences may be different, and the implications of these findings have to be assessed individually.

Of course, these conclusions require qualification. Price increases in the last three years have been accompanied by other changes that may have altered the way people think about educational quality and value; for example, price discounting practices have become more common. Also, Carleton's prospective student pool may have shifted in some subtle way, or differences in the way we constructed our sample and asked for magnitude estimates may have altered the outcome.

Carleton's Primary Market. For any institution, the maintenance of a balance between price and value is complicated further when two or more markets are being served and when there are major differences in the way price and quality are viewed in those markets. For Carleton, which serves both national and local markets, this complexity is clearly present, and for that reason an assessment of Minnesota, Carleton's largest single market, is always an essential part of Carleton's deliberations about its comprehensive fee.

Past findings have shown that within Minnesota the predominant view of those who express an interest in Carleton but do not apply is that the more expensive schools do not provide quality that is commensurate with their high prices, and the most recent data indicate that this view continues to be very strong. In general, past research has indicated that the prospective students from Minnesota who are most likely to apply and enroll are those whose regard for the educational quality of the high-priced schools is comparatively high (Brodigan and Sullivan, 1985).

For this analysis the state was split into two segments; one consisting of nonapplicants living within the Twin Cities (Minneapolis and St. Paul) area, and the other containing those living elsewhere in the state. While this segmentation is a simple geographical one, it is of particular interest because of the contrast between those areas in economic and social conditions. The major difference is that the metropolitan area is thriving and growing, while the farming and mining communities across the state have been experiencing economic difficulty in recent years.

Because of its strong position as a public institution within the educational markets of Minnesota, the University of Minnesota was included in the analysis of Carleton's primary market. Previous research at Carleton has shown that the university is held in high esteem by Minnesota's prospective college students and that it is a strong competitor when measured in terms of the number of applications it receives from Minnesota students (Litten, Sullivan, and Brodigan, 1983).

Our most recent findings regarding perceived price in Minnesota are shown in Figure 5. The two lines represent the least squares best fit for the two groups. The slope of the unbroken line, representing the Twin Cities group, is 0.93. The slope of the broken line, 0.63 (data points not displayed), falls far short. That difference can be attributed, first, to the tendency of members of the Twin Cities group to perceive substantially larger differences between the price of the university and the prices of independent institutions and, second, to their tendency to see slightly larger price differences among the schools in the national, independent category. Among nonapplicants who reside outside of the Twin Cities area, the general tendency is to attribute lower relative sizes to the price differences between institutions. By itself, this set of findings is of considerable interest, but the implications cannot be fully appreciated until the perceptual responses to quality have been examined.

Figure 5. Price Perception of Minnesota Nonapplicants

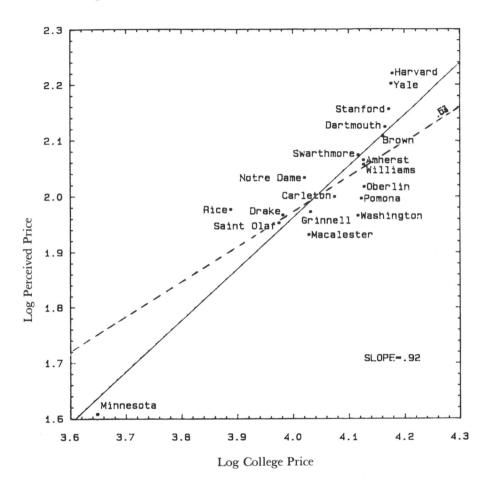

Log College Price

The relationships between perceived price and quality among Minnesotans are displayed in Figure 6. There is very little overall difference between the Twin Cities group and the group living outside of the metropolitan area (the broken line in Figure 6 again represents the least-squares-best-fit line for the second group, points omitted). Both groups attribute nearly as much educational quality to the less expensive schools as they do to the higher-priced ones. For marketing purposes, these findings are very instructive. First, the Twin Cities residents are fairly well informed regarding the costs associated with various institutions, and for them the difference in price between the university and the more expensive colleges is very large. The major challenge for Carleton, in this market, is to raise its level of perceived educational quality.

Figure 6. Price and Quality Perception of Minnesota Nonapplicants

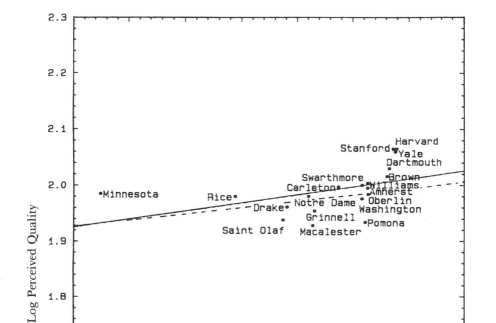

For prospective students living outside the Twin Cities area, the findings are more complex. Not only do members of this group fail to perceive more than modest differences in quality among the institutions lying at various points along the price continuum but they know little about the costs associated with those modest differences. Furthermore, if we assume, for the moment, that the difference in perceived price between the University of Minnesota and the other schools is a psychological representation of the price gap between public and private institutions, we may be surprised to learn that this group, with its smaller gap, had the same probability of enrolling in public schools as members of the Twin Cities group had. In this context, the tuition gap appears not to operate according to the usual expectation that a smaller gap will yield more

88

enrollments in private schools. Based on what we have learned so far, the best explanation for this apparently anomalous result is that the smaller gap arises from a lack of knowledge about college prices and has nothing to do with rational choice between educational options.

For this discussion of Carleton's approach to the problem of balancing price and quality, nonapplicants from outside the Twin Cities present special problems that cannot be directly solved when the fee is set each year. Carleton's public relations and admissions departments should address the problems by speaking to the issues of college education. A simple presentation of information about the availability of financial aid may be of little value when the prospective student knows little about the prices of colleges. The first step, in this case, may be to provide information about the price of admission across the full spectrum of college opportunities.

Conclusion

Magnitude estimation research, aimed at questions of price, quality, and value, can contribute greatly to the understanding and wisdom that are so necessary to careful and thoughtful decisions about institutional fees. At Carleton this kind of research has brought greater understanding of the price and quality issues as they pertain to Carleton's market niche. As has been shown in this chapter, after the basic issues and dynamics are appreciated, this kind of research can produce further refinements in understanding that will aid in decisions involving admissions, marketing, and communications.

Judging from my experience at Carleton, magnitude estimation procedures have considerable potential as an analytic tool in the study of the opportunities available to institutions of higher education. There can be no question that this method of analysis can provide important insights concerning price, quality, and value issues within the prospective student market of a variety of kinds of colleges and universities. Precisely what the results will look like within the admissions markets of institutions with prices closer to the lower end of the continuum, for public institutions, or for schools with strictly regional markets is difficult to predict, but the outcome of that research should be of considerable interest to anyone wishing to acquire a more comprehensive view of the higher education market.

References

Brodigan, D. L. *Admissions Contact Questionnaire.* Northfield, Minn.: Carleton College, April 1986.
Brodigan, D. L., and Sullivan, D. "Perceptions of College Price and Quality." *Journal for Higher Education Management*, 1985, *1*, 19–32.

Litten, L. H. (ed.). *Issues in Pricing Undergraduate Education.* New Directions for Institutional Research, no. 42. San Francisco: Jossey-Bass, 1984.
Litten, L. H., Sullivan, D., and Brodigan, D. L. *Applying Market Research in College Admissions.* New York: College Entrance Examination Board, 1983.
Lodge, M. *Magnitude Scaling.* Beverly Hills, Calif.: Sage, 1981.

David L. Brodigan is director of institutional research at Carleton College, Northfield, Minnesota.

For most institutions, the definition of the key characteristics and needs of student segments influence all subsequent marketing decisions. It is surprising that few institutions make segmentation choices systematically.

Identifying Market Segments

Julie Wakstein

The process of choosing a college is a complex one: A variety of factors play a role in shaping a student's decision to enroll in one institution rather than another. Many of the influences on which research has focused include cost; distance; location; characteristics of students such as ability, gender, ethnicity, and parental education and income; perceptions of image, including strengths and weaknesses of the institution; and recruiting activities, such as publications, interviews, receptions, and campus visits.

From a methodological perspective, analysis of the college choice process is a difficult one. Given that this process is affected by a combination of factors, researchers may employ multivariate techniques such as regression, discriminant, and factor analysis in order to address more appropriately the combined influence of factors. These methods avoid the danger of oversimplification in univariate and bivariate analyses, and often uncover important influences that may otherwise have gone undetected.

Even these sophisticated techiques have limitations, however, and may not appropriately address the subtleties involved in the college choice process. In fact, a great deal of evidence suggests that the impact of influential factors varies at each stage of admissions recruiting and that subgroups of the marketplace do not necessarily respond to these influences similarly. This concept has become known as the "3 *M*'s Principle." Briefly stated, in order for an institution to communicate effectively with its constituen-

R. S. Lay and J. J. Endo (eds.). *Designing and Using Market Research.*
New Directions for Institutional Research, no. 54. San Francisco: Jossey-Bass, Summer 1987.

cies, the right messages must be disseminated to the most receptive markets using the best media.

Market segmentation is one analytical method useful in determining which messages would be most effective for a particular market (see Litten, 1979). This approach helps an institution identify the kinds of students it is most successful in attracting, and to become more sensitive to these differences in students' needs, desires, and perceptions of the institution that have the most impact on their choice of college. Market segmentation methods are invaluable for monitoring recruiting initiatives and additionally focusing recruiting efforts to enroll student groups of particular interest such as certain ethnic groups, women, high-ability students, and students interested in particular academic programs.

Marketing opportunities are much easier to spot once an institution is aware of the distinct subgroups within its marketplace. Armed with this information, institutions can make refinements in programs, if necessary, in order to match student needs and desires and to formulate differentiated communication strategies that hold the most promise for effectively recruiting different types of desired students.

The Chi-Square Automatic Interaction Detector

A systematic exploratory technique that has been used to successfully identify market segments is CHAID, CHi-square Automatic Interaction Detector. This analytic technique has been used primarily by market researchers in the commercial sector. For example, the Ford Motor Company uses CHAID to identify segments of nonbuyers that may require new promotional initiatives to make them more responsive to Ford products. The National Geographic Society employs CHAID to determine its most receptive market segments for direct mail promotions (Mammarella, 1986). Only recently has CHAID begun to establish itself as a useful method for market segmentation in the area of higher education in general and in enrollment management in particular (Lay, Maguire, and Litten, 1982; Lay and Maguire, 1983).

Advantages of CHAID. The CHAID algorithm was first introduced by Kass (1980), and it identifies interactions among factors using a unique branching approach. Unlike other "straight-line" multivariate techniques, such as discriminant, regression, and factor analysis, CHAID has the power to uncover interactions that may have significant influences on one subgroup of the population but not on others. Unlike earlier interaction detecting algorithms, CHAID is more appropriately designed for the exploratory analysis of categorical data because it utilizes the chi-square statistic to measure the combined effects of predictor variables, and it automatically tracks every interaction between them (Magidson, 1982). A major advantage of CHAID is the simplicity of its method. Since the output is expressed in percentages and is displayed via tree diagrams, the results are easily comprehended, even by those unfamiliar with statistics.

How CHAID Operates. Instead of measuring the effects of a predictor variable over the entire group or population sample, CHAID traces the influences through subgroupings that branch independently of one another. For example, in determining the factors that contribute to a high level of student satisfaction, it may be that males are more likely to be satisfied with their college experience if they are academically successful. In contrast, satisfaction among women may relate more to successfully developing a mentor relationship with a member of the faculty.

CHAID operates by searching all the predictors that are eligible for inclusion and tests all the possible splits among the categories of each predictor variable. The resulting splits are those that produce the greatest statistically significant differences among categories. The variable selected for segmentation is the one that exhibits the greatest difference. CHAID tests all possible combinations of categories of a predictor variable against the dependent measure. For example, a variable with four categories can result in as few as two segments, or as many as four segments if each category exhibits significant differences on the dependent measure. If the variable is declared as monotonic, only adjacent categories are considered for merging. However, if the variable is "free," or nominal, the number of possible combinations greatly increases, since categories are permitted to be merged without regard to order.

Segmenting a Pool of Inquirers

Enrollment management research has most commonly concentrated on the pool of accepted applicants. The measurable differences between nonmatriculants and matriculants on both individual characteristics of students and perceptions offer a wealth of information to enrollment planners. Although this transitional stage in the admissions process is certainly a crucial one, one segment of the market that has often been overlooked is that of inquirers. Evaluation of this larger group of students provides institutions with an earlier view of the choice process that may yield a practical strategy for increasing the conversion rate from inquirer to applicant. In a case study of University X, this chapter summarizes the application of a software called SI-CHAID (Statistical Innovations, 1986) to a pool of inquirers in order to illustrate the insight that can be gained from market segmentation.

Data Sources. The data used in this analysis are from a 1985 telephone survey of 491 high school students (most of them seniors) who had requested information from University X. Included in the information elicited from inquirers were demographic characteristics and their ratings on a number of factors that students typically consider when evaluating prospective colleges.

94

Table 1. Variables Eligible for Inclusion

Variable	Definition	Description
COOP	Cooperative education	Evaluation of importance
ACCESS_CITY	Access to a large city	of these characteristics
LOCATION	Geographic location	on a 1–5 scale:
HOUSING	Available housing	n = not at all important
PARKING	Available parking	s = slightly important
CLOSE	Close to home	m = moderately important
SPIRIT	School spirit	v = very important
SOCIAL_LIFE	Social life	e = extremely important
REPUTATION	Academic reputation	
Q_MAJOR	Quality of major	
CONTACT	Close contact with faculty	
R_ATHLETICS	Recreational athletics	
PREP_GRAD	Preparation for graduate or professional school	
SAFE	Safe environment	
ATT_CAMPUS	Attractive campus	
COST	Total cost	
S_BODY	Small student body	
FACILITIES	Academic facilities	
V_ATHLETICS	Varsity athletics	
THE_CITY	Location of institution	Evaluation of desirability on a 1–5 scale: l = highly undesirable u = somewhat undesirable n = neutral d = somewhat desirable h = highly desirable
SEX	Sex of respondent	m = male, f = female
MILES	Distance from institution	c = 1–25 miles 2 = 26–50 miles 3 = 51–150 miles 4 = 151–300 miles 5 = 301–500 miles 6 = 501–1000 miles f = more than 1000 miles
MAJOR	Intended major	b = business e = engineering d = architecture-design a = arts and sciences m = medical o = other u = undecided x = missing data

Table 1. *(continued)*

Variable	Definition	Description
RANK	High school class rank	1 = top 1%
		2 = top 5%
		3 = top 10%
		4 = top 25%
		5 = top 50%
		6 = top 75%
		7 = bottom 25%

Dependent Measures. The dependent measure is the likelihood that an inquirer will submit an application to University X. Inquirers were asked, "What are the chances that you will apply to University X?" The response categories ranged from 1 to 7, where 1 = definitely would not, 2 = probably would not, 3 = possibly would not, 4 = not sure, 5 = possibly will, 6 = probably will, and 7 = definitely will. In order to make the analysis more manageable, responses were collapsed into two categories, likely applicants (possibly will to definitely will apply) and unlikely applicants (not sure to definitely would not apply). Throughout this analysis, the ratio between likely and unlikely applicants is referred to as the *application yield*.

Independent Measures. The variables eligible for inclusion in this analysis are listed in Table 1. Inquirers were asked for demographic information, and they were asked to rate in importance twenty-six institutional characteristics. Response bias was reduced by asking students their opinions on college choice before they knew the identity of the particular institution conducting the survey.

Interpretation of the Findings

Model 1. In Model 1 (see Figure 1), approximately half of the 491 surveyed inquirers expressed some probability of submitting an application to University X. At the first iteration, CHAID identifies the importance of cooperative education as the best predictor of application and determines the optimal splits to be among three subgroups or segments. The lowest application yield (38.2 percent) is among the first subgroup of inquirers (segment A), who view cooperative education as either not at all, (n), slightly, (s), or moderately (m) important. The moderate yield group, (segment B) the second subgroup, is composed of inquirers who consider cooperative education very important (v) (56.7 percent) and increases the overall yield by almost 7 percentage points. The third segment (segment C), the high-yield group, comprises inquirers who rate cooperative education as extremely important (e).

This clearly indicates that cooperative education is a major strength of University X and plays a prominent role in converting inquirers into

96

Figure 1. Model 1: SI-CHAID Analysis of Inquirers— Predicts Likely Applicants

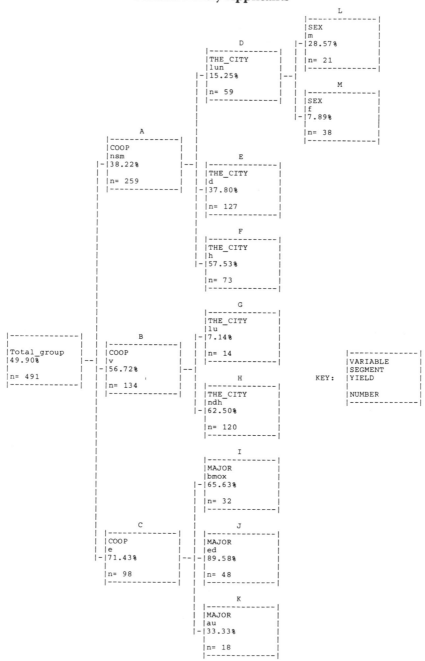

Note: See Table 1 for definitions and variables eligible for inclusion. SI-CHAID® is a registered trademark of Statistical Innovations Inc.

applicants. This distinctive feature, which provides University X with a significant edge over the competition, should be fully appreciated and utilized in order to attract a greater number of students who place a high value on cooperative education. Prospective applicants should be made aware of the availability of the cooperative education program and its educational benefits through intensified marketing and promotion. These efforts might be directed toward a combination of heightening visibility and increasing student interest in the cooperative education program.

The branching pattern from each initial subgroup or segment identifies other high-yield groups that have important marketing implications for University X. For example, this CHAID analysis provides insight into how University X can attract applicants who may not place a high value on the cooperative education experience. The second iteration reveals that the desirability of the city in which University X is located provides the optimal split on both the low-yield and moderate-yield groups (Segments A and B). For the low-yield group, desirability of the city is divided into three segments. Inquirers who view cooperative education as relatively unimportant but perceive the city as highly desirable produce an acceptably high yield.

This relationship is similar in the moderate-yield group, the second subgroup (segment B). However, in this instance, a fairly high application yield results if inquirers view the location of University X as something other than undesirable. In other words, as the importance of cooperative education increases, the perceived desirability of the city becomes less important in influencing application.

Overall, these two segments (F and H) suggest that University X would be more successful in attracting students who may not have a strong preference for cooperative education by identifying itself more closely with the city and by stressing the cultural and recreational advantages that it has to offer. In fact, this particular city had just recently been promoted as an attractive place to live. It would be beneficial to incorporate this point into University X's publications and to emphasize the city's attractiveness in other admissions activities.

The branching on the high-yield group, the third subgroup, indicates a different pattern. The factor that produces the greatest optimal splits on the high-yield group is not the city but rather the intended program of study. The variation in application yield among these segments reflects a difference in the success and availability of cooperative education in each of the programs. It is not surprising that the highest yield is among inquirers who are interested in engineering (e) and architectural design (d), since cooperative education is more fully developed and readily available in these two programs. In fact, cooperative education is mandatory in many of the specific majors within these programs.

It is interesting that the yield for business (b) majors and those relating to medicine and health (m) is not as high as it is for engineering (e) and architectural design (d) majors (segment J) even though cooperative education is also available in these programs. However, cooperative education is not available for all majors within these programs, and it is not as fully integrated. It would appear that if University X were to expand its cooperative education program in these areas, both of which are well suited to such a program, it could enhance its attractiveness among these types of students.

It is more difficult to gauge whether this strategy would be as successful in the recruitment of arts and sciences majors, since many of these specific majors are less career-oriented and thus may be less applicable to cooperative education. In fact, currently, cooperative education is optional in only a few of the specific majors within this school. Although the expansion of cooperative education into the school of arts and science might increase application yield, a program analysis is necessary to determine if this strategy would be cost effective. These data show that only a small group of arts and science majors view cooperative education as extremely important. Although plausible, no direct evidence suggests that these students would be more inclined to apply if cooperative education were available. More research would be necessary to first determine if the desire for such a program could be cultivated among prospective arts and science students.

Model 2. Model 2 (see Figure 2) involves the same set of variables as our first analysis in Model 1, but it illustrates how SI-CHAID can be directed to address a particular issue. In other words, the SI-CHAID software features an interactive mode in which the researcher can exert control over what predictors are selected for segmentation at each iteration. In this example, intended program, which also exhibits substantial differences in yields between segments, is forced into the model as the first predictor in order to explore what motivates inquirers in each of the various fields of study to apply to University X.

Again cooperative education is important to the application yield of all programs except the arts and sciences. Since the perceived importance of cooperative education appears as the best predictor of application for majors in business, medicine, and education (segments A and B), this is further evidence of the competitive edge of University X in drawing these students. Also, since segment G is considerably higher in yield than segment E, this again suggests the need to increase applications by increasing the emphasis on the cooperative education program in the areas of business and medicine.

Two other high-yield groups are produced in the third iteration stemming from segment A. Among business and medicine majors who view cooperative education as relatively unimportant (segment D), the yield increases to approximately 60 percent among inquirers who live

Figure 2. Model 2: SI-CHAID Analysis of Inquirers—
Predicts Likely Applicants

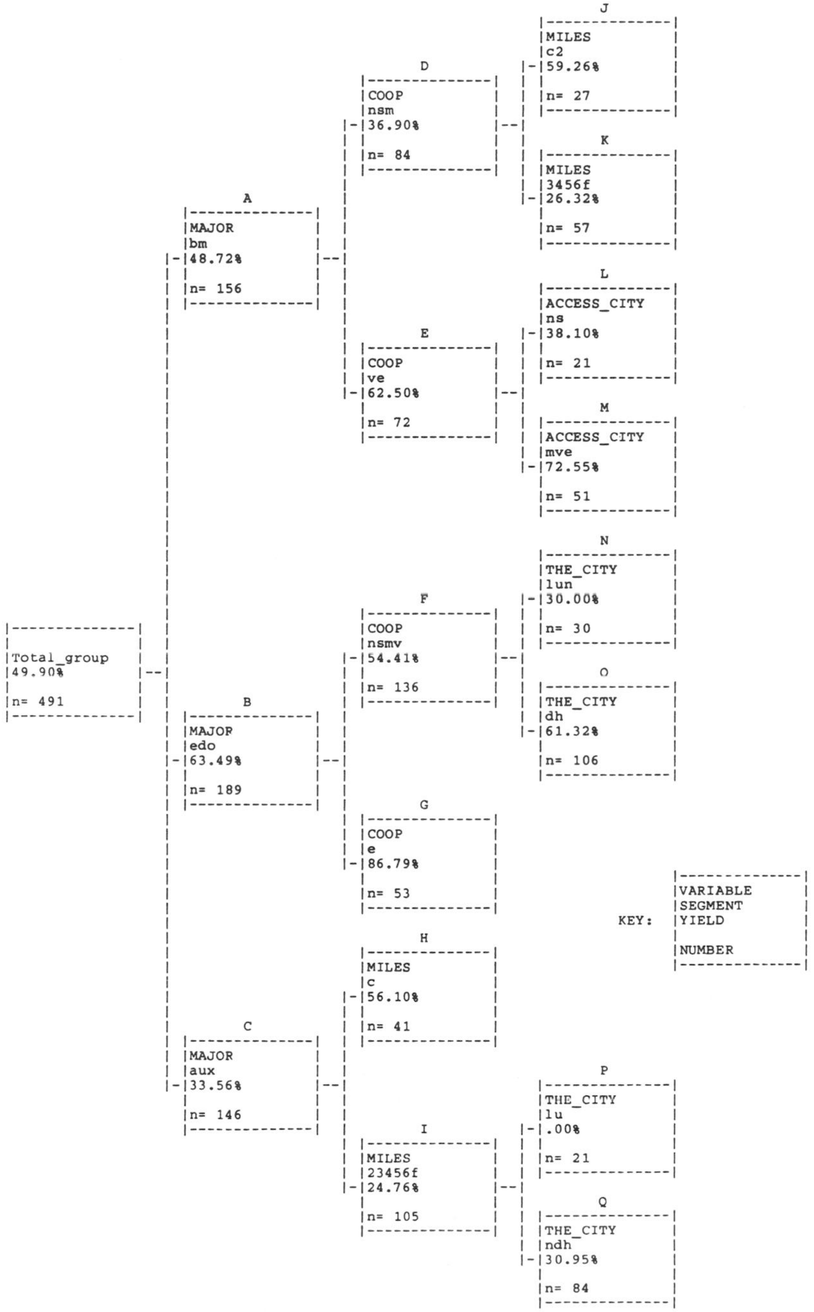

```
                                                          J
                                                 |--------------|
                                                 |MILES         |
                                                 |c2            |
                                        D        |-|59.26%      |
                               |--------------|  | |            |
                               |COOP          |  | |n= 27       |
                               |nsm           |  | |------------|
                               |-|36.90%      |--|
                               | |            |  |       K
                               | |n= 84       |  | |--------------|
                               | |------------|  | |MILES         |
                A              |                 | |3456f         |
        |--------------|       |                 |-|26.32%       |
        |MAJOR         |       |                 | |             |
        |bm            |       |                 | |n= 57        |
        |-|48.72%      |--|    |                 | |-------------|
        | |            |  |    |
        | |n= 156      |  |    |                        L
        | |------------|  |    |                 |--------------|
        |                 |    |                 |ACCESS_CITY   |
        |                 |    |       E         |ns            |
        |                 |    | |--------------||-|38.10%      |
        |                 |    | |COOP          || |            |
        |                 |    | |ve            || |n= 21       |
        |                 |    |-|62.50%        |--|------------|
        |                 |    | |              || |      M
        |                 |    | |n= 72         || |--------------|
        |                 |    | |--------------|| |ACCESS_CITY   |
        |                 |    |                 | |mve           |
        |                 |    |                 |-|72.55%       |
        |                 |    |                 | |             |
        |                 |    |                 | |n= 51        |
        |                 |    |                 | |-------------|
        |                 |
        |                 |                             N
        |                 |                      |--------------|
        |                 |                      |THE_CITY      |
        |                 |             F        |1un           |
        |                 |    |--------------|  |-|30.00%      |
|--------------|          |    |COOP          |  | |            |
|Total_group   |          |    |nsmv          |  | |n= 30       |
|49.90%        |--|       |    |-|54.41%      |--|--------------|
|              |  |       |    | |            |  |       O
|n= 491        |  |       |    | |n= 136      |  | |--------------|
|--------------|  |       |    | |------------|  | |THE_CITY      |
                  |    B   |                     | |dh            |
                  | |--------------|             |-|61.32%       |
                  | |MAJOR         |             | |             |
                  | |edo           |             | |n= 106       |
                  |-|63.49%        |--|          | |-------------|
                  | |              |  |
                  | |n= 189        |  |                 G
                  | |--------------|  |          |--------------|
                  |                   |          |COOP          |
                  |                   |          |e             |
                  |                   |          |-|86.79%      |
                  |                   |          | |            |
                  |                   |          | |n= 53       |     |--------------|
                  |                   |          | |------------|     |VARIABLE      |
                  |                   |                          KEY: |SEGMENT       |
                  |                   |                 H             |YIELD         |
                  |                   |          |--------------|     |              |
                  |                   |          |MILES         |     |NUMBER        |
                  |                   |          |c             |     |--------------|
                  |                   |          |-|56.10%      |
                  |     C             |          | |            |
                  | |--------------|  |          | |n= 41       |
                  | |MAJOR         |  |          | |------------|
                  | |aux           |  |
                  |-|33.56%        |--|                 P
                  | |              |  |          |--------------|
                  | |n= 146        |  |          |THE_CITY      |
                  | |--------------|  |          |1u            |
                  |                   |    I     |-|.00%        |
                  |                   | |--------------|| |            |
                  |                   | |MILES         || |n= 21       |
                  |                   | |23456f        || |------------|
                  |                   |-|24.76%        |--|      Q
                  |                   | |              || |--------------|
                  |                   | |n= 105        || |THE_CITY      |
                  |                   | |--------------|| |ndh           |
                  |                                    |-|30.95%       |
                  |                                    | |             |
                  |                                    | |n= 84        |
                  |                                    | |-------------|
```

Note: See Table 1 for definitions and variables eligible for inclusion. SI-CHAID® is a registered trademark of Statistical Innovations Inc.

within fifty miles of the institution (segment J). Therefore it may be advantageous for the admissions office to cultivate interest in students who live in the area. An even higher yield is evident among those who rate cooperative education highly (segment M), reinforcing the idea that access to the city is important in the application decisions among inquirers of University X.

The branching from the low-yield subgroup of arts and sciences majors (segment C), is particularly informative. Although cooperative education did not emerge as a predictor variable among arts and sciences majors, this may be due to the almost total absence of cooperative education in this school. If the emphasis on cooperative education remains unchanged in this program, it may be that the best way to increase applications is by concentrating more heavily on local students (those that live within twenty-five miles of the institution).

Implications

The diagrams resulting from a CHAID analysis makes it a rather simple task to track outcomes and evaluate strategies. And as with most good research, CHAID stimulates thought and identifies areas that warrant further investigation. However, beyond the valuable information that can be inferred from this type of analysis, CHAID has the added advantage that it is straightforward and relatively easy to understand. This is particularly important, since the persons responsible for conducting the research are often not the same as those responsible for making policy decisions. The simplicity of CHAID's method, ease of interpretation, and presentation of results allow for optimal transfer of information between researcher and planner.

The CHAID analyses presented here demonstrate how an institution can apply market segmentation to a group of inquirers in order to learn more about its image and distinguish between distinct subgroups of the market that merit separate strategies for communication and program development. Segmentation analysis also has practical applications to other constituencies such as current students, dropouts, alumni, parents, and high school counselors. A variety of approaches can be implemented in the evaluation of these groups. Segmentation analysis is a creative act. Its uses and applications are numerous and limited only by the imagination of the researcher.

References

Kass, G. "An Exploratory Technique for Investigating Large Quantities of Categorical Data." *Applied Statistics*, 1980, *29*, 119–127.

Lay, R. S., and Maguire, J. *Computer Aided Segmentation Analysis: New Software* for *College Admissions Marketing*. Skokie, Ill.: National Association of College Admissions Counselors, 1983.

Lay, R. S., Maguire, J., and Litten, L. "Identifying Distinctive Groups in a College Applicant Pool." *Research in Higher Education*, 1982, *16* (3), 195–207.

Litten, L. "Market Structure and Institutional Position in Geographic Market Segments." *Research in Higher Education*, 1979, *2*, 59–83.

Magidson, J. "Some Common Pitfalls in Causal Analysis of Categorical Data." *Journal of Marketing Researrch*, 1982, *14*, 461–471.

Mammarella, J. "Psyching out List Overlays." *Direct Marketing*, 1986, *48* (11), 46.

Statistical Innovations, Inc. SI-CHAID. Belmont, Mass.: Statistical Innovations, Inc., 1986.

Julie Wakstein is director of research at Enrollment Management Consultants in Concord, Massachusetts.

This chapter describes the development and implementation of a marketing plan that focuses on the recruitment of new freshmen. A case study based on the University of Colorado at Boulder illustrates the major planning considerations.

Developing and Implementing a Marketing Plan

Byron G. McCalmon

Successful marketing requires the careful development and implementation of a marketing plan. Marketing plans vary widely in scope and purpose and institutions typically work with several simultaneously. This chapter describes the development and implementation of a marketing plan that focuses on the recruitment of new freshmen. A case study based on the University of Colorado at Boulder illustrates the major planning considerations.

Developing a Marketing Plan

The formal development of a marketing plan actually incorporates many of the elements of strategic planning, and the following discussion makes use of certain strategic planning concepts (Jedamus, Peterson, and Associates, 1980; Cope, 1978; Steiner, 1979). The initial development of a marketing plan should include the following steps: (1) a situation analysis, (2) development of goals and objectives, (3) design of marketing strategies and programs, and (4) preparation of a budget.

Conducting a Situation Analysis. A situation analysis involves making assessments of the internal and external environments of an institution. From these assessments key marketing issues are identified. While

R. S. Lay and J. J. Endo (eds.). *Designing and Using Market Research.*
New Directions for Institutional Research, no. 54. San Francisco: Jossey-Bass, Summer 1987.

such assessments are being made it is also useful to determine the amount of time and effort that is needed to complete a marketing plan.

In assessing the internal environment of an institution, its strengths and weaknesses as well as enrollment patterns over time by program (numbers of applicants, acceptances, and enrollments), student background and academic characteristics, retention and graduation rates, and students' satisfaction with their educational experiences and programs could be examined. When assessing the external environment, attention could be focused on obtaining answers to such broad questions as: (1) What are the needs, perceptions, and expectations of applicants who are interested in enrolling? (2) Which institutions compete for the same applicants? (3) How satisfied are applicants with specific recruitment programs? and (4) What factors distinguish between applicants who enroll at a particular institution and those who do not?

During these environmental assessments, relevant data will have to be collected and analyzed. Some data will be available from an institution's operational data bases and various institutional offices or reports. However, important information gaps may have to be filled by undertaking special market research studies.

The amount of time and effort that an institution puts into completing a marketing plan will depend on the importance and extent of its enrollment problems and the complexity of its student markets. But almost as important is a realistic assessment of how useful a plan will be within the institution. It is foolish to devote six months to developing a plan that no one will use. A marketing plan should usually be written by or for the institutional decision maker who will implement and evaluate the results of the plan.

Developing Goals and Objectives. A situation analysis provides the basis for setting the goals and objectives of a marketing plan. Goals are broad, abstract statements that describe ideal outcomes. To be able to gauge progress toward achieving goals, objectives must be established that can be measured. Goals and objectives must be related to the broad mission statement of an institution and to the priorities of the admissions office. The views of various administrative, faculty, and student leaders and other important institutional constituencies should be solicited and incorporated, forming the basis for broader institutional support.

Designing Marketing Strategies and Programs. Goals and objectives should be used to design marketing strategies and programs. A strategy is a plan of action while programs are the specific activities that accomplish a strategy. Most of the creativity of a good marketing plan will be evidenced by this step. The more accurate the situation analysis and the clearer the institutional goals, the greater the likelihood that viable strategies will be developed for achieving set objectives.

Preparing a Budget. The budget for the marketing plan allocates financial resources to various marketing programs. In the budget, programs are prioritized and financial commitments made in the order of their importance. However, when creating budgets, a certain degree of flexibility must be built in in anticipation of unforeseen future changes.

It is important to reemphasize that the success of the plan is contingent on widespread institutional support. This commitment is generated by involving key administrators, faculty and student leaders, student affairs and research offices, alumni, and academic units, especially those with special recruitment needs or activities of their own. Ideally, such involvement will generate an atmosphere of cooperation in which all parties feel a stake in the success of the plan, provide political support, and offer resources to help implement the plan. Such involvement will also have other benefits, including improved intracampus communication, an increased sensitivity to recruitment matters, and a better understanding of the work of the admissions office by all participants.

A Case Study: The University of Colorado

Some of the preceding discussion can be illustrated by examining the development of a marketing plan at the University of Colorado at Boulder (henceforth referred to as Boulder). Boulder is a comprehensive public institution whose instructional mission is to offer a broad curriculum in the arts, sciences, humanities, and the professions, ranging from the baccalaureate through the doctoral level. At Boulder marketing activities are coordinated by the associate vice-chancellor for academic services and the Office of Admissions.

An assessment of Boulder's external environment points up a number of significant factors. For example, the state of Colorado has experienced positive growth over the past ten years, but the state legislature has limited enrollment growth at Boulder. For several years, the number of resident students has been limited to 13,600 full-time equivalents (FTE). This has forced Boulder to turn away qualified resident applicants and to more actively recruit nonresident students.

An assessment of Boulder's internal environment also identifies several important concerns, including those related to the number of applications, acceptances, and enrollments. Boulder has had many more qualified applicants in recent years than available positions for both residents and nonresidents. Moreover, while Boulder hopes to matriculate freshman classes of about 45 percent nonresidents and 55 percent residents, it receives about two thousand more applications annually from the former than from the latter. However, the ratio of admitted students to matriculated ones is lower for nonresidents than for residents.

As assessments of Boulder's external and internal environments were being made, information gaps were identified. Some of these gaps were addressed in special market research studies (Endo and others, 1982; Endo, McCalmon, Lynn, and Storey, 1984; Lynn, Endo, McCalmon, and Storey, 1984) conducted on Boulder's applicant pool. The assessments of the internal and external environment contributed to the development of marketing plan goals and objectives. These are too extensive to describe here, but one objective was to increase the number and confirmation rate of nonresident applicants in the face of increased recruiting efforts by other institutions and the declining numbers of potential college students in such states as California, New York, and Illinois, from which Boulder traditionally draws large numbers of students. Several strategies and programs were designed around this objective (as well as others). Some of the strategies were to:

- Target recruitment activities at geographical regions that have the largest numbers of nonresident applicants
- Direct recruitment activities toward the parents of prospective nonresident applicants
- Mail financial aid award letters early to maximize confirmation rates
- Encourage prospective students and their parents to visit the campus.

Some of the programs directed toward the parents of prospective nonresident applicants included:

- Developing a newsletter that describes academic, cultural, and social programs
- Establishing a volunteer group of parents of current students to help with recruitment activities
- Setting up special events to encourage prospective students and their parents to visit the campus.

Many strategies and programs made use of the results of Boulder's market research studies. For instance, in two of these studies (Endo and others, 1982; Endo, McCalmon, Lynn, and Storey, 1984), multivariate analyses showed that parents' support for their children attending Boulder, being offered financial aid, and a visit to the Boulder campus were related to nonresident respondents' decisions to attend. In addition, information found by research to be important to parents (on such issues as housing, access to high-demand programs, quality of undergraduate instruction, student-faculty interaction, and quality of facilities and equipment) was incorporated into various recruitment-oriented publications. Research results along with census data were also used to identify new student markets that had characteristics similar to those of traditional or proven markets.

Boulder's marketing plan also included a budget. Recruiting nonresident students was constrained by available resources, and out-of-state activities often necessitated expensive travel to regions far from Colorado.

This and similar constraints required careful review of specific programs concerned with such recruitment (as well as others).

Implementation of a Marketing Plan

Implementation involves organizing activities, allocating resources, making personnel assignments, training and motivating staff members and volunteers, and maintaining a cooperative, supportive climate for marketing activities at an institution. In a general sense, implementation is a fairly straightforward matter that will vary depending on circumstances at each institution—and that will be complicated by unforeseen events and extenuating circumstances. The following are some things to consider in implementing a marketing plan:

1. The implementation of a marketing plan should involve more than just the admissions office, in order to maximize limited personnel and financial resources and to maintain the political support and cooperative atmosphere generated during the development of the plan. Though marketing should be seen as the responsibility of everyone who comes into contact with prospective students and their parents, in actuality, certain units will be the most heavily involved, including academic departments, student affairs offices that come into daily contact with students such as counseling and registration, and offices that have an understanding of enrollment management concerns, such as the budget, finance, and publications offices.

2. Similarly, marketing programs should make use of a wide variety of persons, including the professional student affairs staff and volunteers— students, parents, alumni, faculty, administrators, and other institutional staff members.

3. The responsibility for organizing the implementation of a marketing plan must be clearly defined; usually this will reside within the admissions office.

4. Plans must be made for training staff members and volunteers. The professional student affairs staff can be trained in conjunction with everyday admissions-related work. Training of volunteers is harder to accomplish. Preferably, volunteers should be carefully selected and be open, honest, hard-working people who are enthusiastic about the institution and willing to follow flexible schedules. Expectations for volunteers should be kept within reasonable bounds, and most should be given a few clearly defined tasks. Their training should cover the nature of their duties and how these fit into the total marketing plan, updated information on the institution, and in some instances, the rudiments of public speaking.

5. As marketing programs actually get under way, it will be useful to hold periodic group meetings of participants or at least institute regular reporting procedures regarding happenings, problems, and milestones achieved. Frequent communication is essential to keep all participants

informed of progress in other areas, to identify emerging problems, to reduce the chance of misinformation or duplication of effort, to obtain useful feedback on the effectiveness of various programs, and to create a sense of involvement among all participants.

6. As programs are completed, it is important to convene participants for formal critiques. Such critiques can contribute to an overall assessment of the marketing plan as well as provide an important sense of closure for participants.

Implementing a Marketing Plan at the University of Colorado

The implementation of Boulder's marketing plan mainly involves the associate vice-chancellor for academic services, the Office of Admissions, and individuals in the offices of registration and records, budget, bursar, counseling, alumni, and publications. Boulder's main marketing programs focus on recruitment at secondary schools, alumni activities, college fairs, and publications. Recruitment at secondary schools includes sending admissions staff members and other volunteers to high schools in Colorado and designated locations across the country. Alumni activities center on high school visits, participation at college fairs, on-campus events to acquaint prospective students with Boulder's programs and facilities, telephoning accepted applicants, fundraising, and producing a parents' newsletter. Major publications include the Boulder catalogue, a prospective students' brochure that is a brief guide to Boulder and its undergraduate programs, and a "grabber," which is a two-page overview of Boulder for mass distribution, for example, at college fairs and during high school visits.

Apart from these, a larger number of other Boulder offices and people make marketing contributions. For instance, the Office of Academic Computing Services has put together a flier explaining Boulder's computing environment to prospective students, and the engineering dean's office holds several programs aimed at exposing prospective students to Boulder's engineering curriculum. The housing department makes special arrangements to host campus visitors, while the School of Music makes recruitment publications available during their off-campus performances. Academic departments and individual faculty members also make contributions by giving sample lectures for prospective students and their parents on special be-a-student days, by writing descriptive pieces about their course offerings, and by writing or telephoning accepted applicants.

Boulder's marketing efforts even extend to the routine activities of the admissions and financial aid offices. For example, inquiries from prospective students are handled in a timely matter, and customized letters and publications are sent to various subpopulations of prospective students such as minority-group students. In addition, some results from Boulder's market research studies have shown that all contacts with current Boulder students are important in creating a positive impression of the institution, and current students are among the best recruiters of new students. Therefore, a special effort is made to make student services more helpful and efficient.

With the help of the associate vice-chancellor (AVC), the Admissions Office coordinates the implementation of secondary school visits, publications, participation at college fairs, several alumni activities, and marketing programs involving the Admissions Office. Actual organizing for the recruitment of any given fall cohort of new Boulder freshmen begins a year and a half before their matriculation. The AVC meets with the offices of admissions, publications, alumni, and financial aid to discuss general concepts, overall plans, preliminary projections of budgetary needs, and previous marketing experiences. These meetings continue on a weekly basis throughout the recruitment cycle, and they enable the AVC to monitor various programs, incorporate the results of market research studies, assist in problem solving, provide needed resources, and ensure that staff members and volunteers receive proper training. Publications require the longest lead time for preparation of materials; for instance, photographs of particular events or seasons must be taken a year in advance. New marketing programs also require a long lead time.

Approximately six months into the recruitment cycle, resources begin to be allocated, and a number of programs are then set in motion. For example, the format of publications is set, and staff members and other volunteers who will make high school visits and participate in college fairs are selected and trained. High school visits and college fairs are scheduled during the subsequent fall. In the winter, one year into the recruitment cycle, financial aid plans are finalized and implemented, and in the spring and summer volunteers make phone calls to accepted applicants.

Evaluating a Marketing Plan

An institution's marketing efforts do not end with the development and implementation of a marketing plan. An evaluation measures the outcomes of a marketing plan or the degree to which measurable objectives are achieved.

The evaluation of a marketing plan should be taking place continuously. Each step of its development and implementation should be critiqued by relevant participants as it occurs or is completed. These critiques become part of a total evaluation that can be used to modify or create new programs for any subsequent recruitment cycle. A total evaluation should also cover the following:

- Assessments of the application process by current students and applicants who selected alternative institutions
- Assessments of recruitment efforts by secondary school personnel
- Assessments by the staff and volunteers who participated in various marketing programs
- Analyses of application and enrollment trends
- Budget analyses of marketing programs
- Longitudinal studies of students and graduates.

Assessments of the application process by current students and applicants who selected alternative institutions can be conducted using standard survey research techniques. Assessments of recruitment efforts by secondary school personnel might be conducted through face-to-face interviews done in conjunction with high school recruitment visits or through the use of mail questionnaires. These assessments should include questions about recruitment publications, the application process, and any follow-up communications with an institution. Assessments by institutional staff members and volunteers should be done on an ongoing basis during the development and implementation of a marketing plan, as indicated earlier. However, special times might be set aside for this, as appropriate, at the conclusion of various programs.

Analyses of application and enrollment trends should include data from at least five years. These analyses should also examine specific student subgroups targeted in a marketing plan, for instance nonresidents from particular states. Budget analyses of marketing programs should examine cost effectiveness so that the least effective can be replaced. However, budget analyses should also consider resources available for marketing that often have to be estimated months in advance. Longitudinal studies should be conducted of students and graduates to find out whether students who were successfully recruited were satisfied with their educational experiences and achievements. These studies can be done using standard longitudinal survey procedures.

In evaluating a marketing plan, it is important to remember that many objectives cannot be adequately measured after only one year, and longer periods may be necessary to determine whether the intended outcomes actually took place. In addition, it will be difficult to attribute results to any specific marketing program. The most important thing to determine is whether an institution is generally moving toward its desired marketing objectives.

Conclusion

The following are some suggestions for developing and implementing a marketing plan. First, determine whether new marketing initiatives are really necessary by analyzing enrollment trends. Second, if a major commitment to marketing planning is deemed worthwhile, plan on conducting market research studies to fill information gaps. Third, before developing a marketing plan, be aware of internal and external constraints on enrollment. For example, it may make little sense to focus on improving the attractiveness of publications if a high percentage of prospective students will not be able to afford to attend due to federal cutbacks in financial assistance over the next five years. Time may be better allocated to finding new, creative ways of helping students finance their education. Fourth, make use of the ideas and resources of many offices and significant campus constituencies. The successful development and implementation of a marketing plan requires widespread institutional participation.

References

Cope, R. G. *Strategic Policy Planning: A Guide for College and University Administrators.* Littleton, Colo.: Ireland Educational Corporation, 1978.

Endo, J. J., Harpel, R., Bittner, T., Branch, G., Grotewold, D., Johnson, S., McCalmon, B., McKeevee, M., and Parker, V. *Survey of College Choice of Accepted Applicants at the University of Colorado at Boulder, Fall 1981.* Boulder: Office of Academic Planning, University of Colorado, 1982.

Endo, J. J., McCalmon, B., Lynn, J., and Storey, P. *Survey of College Choice of Accepted Applicants at the University of Colorado at Boulder, Fall 1983.* Boulder: Office of Academic Planning, University of Colorado, 1984.

Jedamus, P., Peterson, M. W., and Associates. *Improving Academic Management: A Handbook of Planning and Institutional Research.* San Francisco: Jossey-Bass, 1980.

Lynn, J., Endo, J. J., McCalmon, B., and Storey, P. *Parental Attitudes Toward College Choice, University of Colorado at Boulder, 1983 Survey.* Boulder: Office of Admissions and Office of Academic Planning, University of Colorado, 1984.

Steiner, G. A. *Strategic Planning: What Every Manager Must Know.* New York: Free Press, 1979.

Byron G. McCalmon is associate vice chancellor of student administrative services at the University of Colorado, Boulder. He has worked in the field for twenty-four years at both public and private universities and as a consultant.

The literature on marketing research in higher education is very extensive. This chapter highlights some sources that will be especially useful to newcomers in this field.

Selected References on Market Research in Higher Education

Jean J. Endo, Robert S. Lay

The literature on market research in higher education has grown almost geometrically over the last five years. As published research becomes more complex and more specialized, it becomes difficult for the newcomer to the field to gain a useful perspective on how to adapt techniques and findings to individual campuses. To counteract this tendency toward specialization, we will note a few basic, widely available sources helpful for understanding relationships between the most comprehensive thinking on academic marketing and the best market research for institutions of higher education. A recent, more comprehensive list of references can be found in *An Annotated and Extended Bibliography of Higher Education Marketing* by Karen Constantine (Chicago: American Marketing Association, 1986).

Nonprofit Marketing

Kotler, P. *Marketing for Nonprofit Organizations.* (2nd ed.) Englewood Cliffs, N.J.: Prentice-Hall, 1982.
    This work provides a broad overview of marketing in nonprofit organizations. Kotler describes the nature and relevance of marketing to

R. S. Lay and J. J. Endo (eds.). *Designing and Using Market Research.*
New Directions for Institutional Research, no. 54. San Francisco: Jossey-Bass, Summer 1987.

nonprofit organizations, how to organize a marketing analysis, major concepts and tools available to understand markets and possible strategies, when to try to change the marketing mix, ways to attract resources, and how to adapt general marketing principles to techniques for marketing services, persons, places, and ideas.

Marketing in Higher Education

Kotler, P., and Fox, K.F.A. *Strategic Marketing for Educational Institutions.* Englewood Cliffs, N.J.: Prentice-Hall, 1985.

This work covers the essential elements of marketing for educational institutions. The six sections of the book include understanding marketing, planning marketing, understanding markets, establishing the marketing mix, applying marketing techniques, and evaluating marketing. Kotler and Fox illustrate practical approaches used by several institutions for attracting students, increasing student satisfaction, developing academic programs, and obtaining alumni support.

Conducting Market Research in Higher Education

Litten, L. H., Sullivan, D., and Brodigan, D. L. *Applying Market Research in College Admissions.* New York: College Entrance Examination Board, 1983.

The authors examine a successful market research program at Carleton College and describe a six-market study of San Francisco–Oakland, Denver-Boulder, Dallas–Ft. Worth, Chicago, Minneapolis–St. Paul, and Baltimore–Washington, D.C. A variety of techniques for understanding student markets are presented and several ways to administer college marketing based on these research findings are explored.

Zemsky, R., and Oedel, P. *The Structure of College Choice.* New York: College Entrance Examination Board, 1983.

This work discusses a comprehensive enrollment planning project funded by the College Entrance Examination Board. The authors use their market segmentation model to describe the college choices of a half-million high school seniors in the eastern United States. This model helps institutions measure their visibility within and across various types of college-bound students. Zemsky and Oedel analyze the competition for students between various institutions and discuss the implications for developing recruitment strategies.

Practical Considerations in Higher Education Marketing

Smith, J. *The Admissions Strategist: Recruiting in the 1980s.* New York: College Entrance Examination Board, 1985.

This work is a begins a series of publications edited by the director of the Student Search Service of the College Board. Written by admissions practitioners, the articles are filled with useful ideas on what works (and what does not). Of special interest for academic marketers are volumes that group articles on specific segments such as adults, minority students, and foreign students.

Hossler, D. *Enrollment Management: An Integrated Approach.* New York: College Entrance Examination Board, 1984.

Hossler examines a variety of factors that influence enrollments, and he reviews research findings on the demand for higher education, college choice, pricing and financial aid, student retention, advising, and student outcomes.

Hossler, D. (ed.). *Managing College Enrollments.* New Directions for Higher Education, no. 53. San Francisco: Jossey-Bass, 1986.

This work examines how institutions may exert greater influence over student enrollments. Hossler includes chapters on pricing, student-institution fit, student persistence, student outcomes, the role of administrators, and institutional research in enrollment management.

Jean J. Endo is assistant director in the office of institutional research at the University of Colorado, Boulder. She has designed and conducted research on academic marketing, attrition, student outcomes, and alumni.

Robert S. Lay is dean of enrollment management at Suffolk University in Boston and was director of research at Boston College for eight years.

Index